The Essential Guide to Bread and Sourdough Mastery

Recipes and Techniques for Home Bakers

ALAN COLLINS

Alan Collins

Table of Content

Alan Collins

Introduction:

In life's wonderful realm of food and cooking, few experiences compare to the simplicity, yet profound complexity, of baking bread. The act of transforming humble ingredients—flour, water, salt, and yeast—into a warm, crusty loaf is an event that taps into something primal and profoundly satisfying. *The Definitive Bread and Sourdough Recipe Cookbook* is your comprehensive guide to mastering the art and science of bread and sourdough baking.

This book begins by demystifying the process of bread-making, breaking it down to its most basic elements. Even if you're a complete beginner with no baking experience, you'll gain a solid understanding of the ingredients, equipment, and techniques necessary to create beautiful, tasty loaves. For more experienced bakers, this book will offer fresh insights and innovative methods to push your bread crafting skills to new heights.

The core of the book revolves around the world of sourdough, an ancient method of baking bread that harnesses the power of natural yeast and bacteria to leaven bread. Here, you will explore the intricate science behind sourdough, learn how to cultivate your own sourdough starter, and discover the vast spectrum of flavors and textures that this unique form of bread offers.

Throughout the chapters, we delve into various techniques of kneading, shaping, and scoring, which will allow you to craft a diverse array of bread shapes, from the classic boule to more intricate designs. We will also discuss the keys to achieving the perfect crust and crumb—from the crispy, golden exterior to the soft, airy interior.

Expanding your bread repertoire, we then embark on a journey to explore various types of bread from around the world. We will teach you how to incorporate different grains, flours, and additives into your bread, allowing you to create a multitude of bread types and flavors. From the hearty wholewheat loaf to the delicate, buttery brioche, there's a recipe to suit every palate and occasion.

One unique feature of this book is its approach to bread as a fundamental part of every meal. We will show you how to bake a wide variety of breads that are perfect for breakfast, lunch, dinner, and even dessert. You'll learn how to transform a basic sourdough into a stunning pizza crust, a sweet cinnamon roll, a hearty sandwich loaf, and more.

Lastly, we address the important aspects of storing and preserving your bread to ensure you always have fresh, delicious loaves at your disposal. You'll learn how to freeze dough for future use, how to properly store baked bread, and how to revitalize stale bread.

By the end of this book, you will not only have mastered the art of bread-baking, but you will have also discovered the profound joy and satisfaction that comes from creating beautiful, artisanal bread from scratch.

Chapter 1

The Rise of Bread: Understanding the Basics of Bread-Making

Bread, in its simplest form, consists of four basic ingredients: flour, water, yeast, and salt. Yet, these humble components can create a world of complexity and variety, giving rise to the myriad types of bread found across different cultures and cuisines.

Flour: The Backbone of Bread

Flour provides the structure of your bread. When flour is mixed with water, two proteins present in it—glutenin and gliadin—combine to form gluten. Gluten's unique elastic and stretchable properties are what give bread its structure, enabling it to hold onto the gases produced during fermentation, leading to the bread rising.

Water: The Hydrator and Activator

Water does much more than just moisten the flour. It hydrates the proteins, starches, and enzymes in the flour, which is critical for gluten development and enzymatic reactions. Additionally, water also helps dissolve the yeast and salt.

Yeast: The Leavener

Yeast plays a crucial role in bread- making by serving as a leavening agent. When yeast ferments the sugars present in the flour, it produces carbon dioxide gas and alcohol. The gas gets trapped in the gluten network, causing the bread to rise and contributing to its final volume and texture.

Salt: The Flavor Enhancer and Regulator

While salt might seem like a minor ingredient, its impact on bread are far-reaching. Apart from enhancing flavor, salt also strengthens the gluten network and regulates yeast activity, preventing it from fermenting too rapidly.

The process of bread-making can be broadly categorized into a series of steps:

Mixing: In this initial step, all the ingredients are combined until a dough is formed. This is when gluten starts to develop.

Kneading: The dough is manipulated—either by hand or with a machine—to strengthen the gluten network.

Fermentation or Proofing: The dough is allowed to rest and rise. During this time, yeast ferments the sugars to produce carbon dioxide, which inflates the gluten network and causes the dough to grow in size.

Shaping: The risen dough is deflated and formed into the desired shape.

Second Proofing: The shaped dough undergoes a final rise to achieve the necessary volume.

Baking: The dough is baked until it has fully set and developed a crust.

Cooling: The bread is left to cool, allowing the crumb structure to set.

The Importance of Ingredients

While following these steps making bread is essential, the quality of your ingredients can significantly impact your final product. Here, we will discuss why sourcing high-quality ingredients can elevate your bread-making process and outcome.

Quality flour is key to good bread. For most bread types, you will want to use bread flour or all-purpose flour, both of which have a moderate protein content optimal for gluten development. Whole wheat and rye flours have a lower gluten-forming protein content but offer more flavor and nutrition. Different flours will have different levels of moisture absorption and require adjustments in the amount of water added.

Water quality can also affect your bread. Tap water treated with chlorine can inhibit yeast activity, making filtered or bottled water a better choice for bread-making. The temperature of the water is also vital; warmer water will speed up yeast activity, while colder water will slow it down.

When it comes to yeast, ensure it's fresh for maximum activity. There are different types of yeast available: active dry yeast, instant yeast, and fresh yeast. While they all serve the same purpose, they require different handling and quantities. Active dry yeast needs to be dissolved in water before use, while instant yeast can be mixed directly into the flour. Fresh yeast, also known as cake yeast, is highly perishable and needs to be used shortly after purchase.

Salt should be added with care, as too much can kill the yeast and inhibit gluten development. Stick to the recommended quantity in the recipe. Avoid using iodized salt as it can lend a metallic taste to your bread. Instead, opt for kosher or sea salt.

The Art of Mixing and Kneading
When you begin mixing your ingredients, start slow. Adding water gradually allows the flour to absorb it evenly. Mixing too aggressively from the start can result in a dough that is uneven and difficult to work with.

Once your dough has come together, the kneading process begins. Kneading develops gluten, the protein structure that gives bread its characteristic chew and structure. The goal is a dough that is smooth, elastic, and slightly tacky. Over kneading can lead to a dough that is tough and dense, while under-kneading can result in a dough that doesn't hold its shape well.

The Science of Fermentation

Fermentation, also known as proofing, is where your dough transforms. This stage is when the yeast consumes the sugars in your dough, creating carbon dioxide gas and alcohol. The gas inflates the gluten network, causing your dough to rise, while the alcohol contributes to the flavor of your bread.

Fermentation time depends on several factors including the amount of yeast used, the temperature of your dough, and the ambient temperature.

You'll know your dough has finished its first proofing when it has approximately doubled in size.

Remember, bread making is as much an art as it is a science. It requires patience, practice, and some intuition, which you will develop over time.

Shaping Your Bread

Shaping your bread is more than just a matter of aesthetics; it's a crucial step that influences the final texture and crumb of your loaf. During shaping, you create tension on the surface of the dough that helps it maintain its form during the final rise and baking. Additionally, the way you shape your loaf can affect the distribution of bubbles in your bread, leading to different crumb structures.

There are many ways to shape your bread, depending on the type of bread you are making. For a basic round loaf or "boule," the dough is turned on the work surface using lightly floured hands until a smooth, tight ball is formed. For a "batard" or an oblong loaf, the dough is first shaped into a rectangle, then folded and sealed to create surface tension.

The Second Rise: Building Flavor and Volume

After shaping, the dough undergoes a second rise, also known as "proofing." This step is critical for developing the final texture and flavor of the bread. During this stage, fermentation continues, allowing the yeast to produce more carbon dioxide gas and alcohol. The dough should increase in volume by about half, and it should feel light and full of air.

A common way to check if the dough has proofed enough is the "poke test." If you gently poke the dough with a floured finger and the indentation slowly springs back, the dough is ready to bake. If it springs back immediately, it needs more time. And if the dough doesn't spring back at all, it has over-proofed.

Baking Your Bread: Creating the Perfect Crust and Crumb

The final transformation occurs in the oven. As the bread bakes, the heat causes the yeast to work in overdrive, creating a rapid burst of gas in a phenomenon known as "oven spring." This causes the bread to rise dramatically in the first few minutes of baking.

At the same time, the heat causes the water in the dough to turn into steam, which gelatinizes the starches on the surface of the bread, forming a crust. The steam also keeps the crust soft for longer, allowing the bread to expand fully before the crust hardens.

The internal temperature of the bread should reach around 190-210°F (88-99°C) when it's done. The bread should have a golden-brown crust and sound hollow when tapped on the bottom.

Cooling and Storing Your Bread

Once out of the oven, resist the temptation to cut into your hot loaf immediately. As the bread cools, the steam inside it continues to migrate outward, setting the final crumb structure. Cutting into hot bread can result in a gummy texture.

After the bread has fully cooled, store it in a breadbox or paper bag. Avoid storing bread in the refrigerator, which can make it stale more quickly. If you won't eat the bread within a few days, consider freezing it.

The Fascinating History of Bread

Now that we've covered the mechanics of bread-making, let's take a moment to appreciate the rich history of this staple food. The invention of bread has been so crucial to human development that it's often considered one of the cornerstones of civilization.

The earliest bread, dating back about 14,000 years, was more akin to flatbread and was made from wild grains and water. The grains were ground into flour, mixed with water, and then baked on hot stones. The invention of leavened bread didn't come until around 6,000 years ago when Egyptians discovered that dough left to sit would rise and result in a lighter, airier bread.

Bread's importance in society is reflected in its prevalence in religious and cultural rituals worldwide, symbolizing everything from spiritual nourishment to prosperity. Having a sense of this history can add a new layer of appreciation for the simple act of baking bread.

Wheat Varieties and Their Effects on Bread

There are numerous varieties of wheat, each of which can lend different characteristics to your bread. For instance, hard wheat has a high protein content and is ideal for bread-making, thanks to its robust gluten-forming potential. Soft wheat, on the other hand, has lower protein content and is typically used for pastries and cakes.

In recent years, ancient grains like spelt, kamut, and einkorn have seen a resurgence in popularity. These grains have a different flavor profile and nutritional content compared to modern wheat, offering bakers more options for experimentation.

Other Grains in Bread-Making
While wheat is the most common grain used in bread, it's by no means the only one. Rye, barley, corn, and oats are also frequently used in bread-making, each contributing its unique flavor and texture characteristics.

Rye, for instance, has a deep, earthy flavor but a lower gluten content, making rye bread denser than wheat bread. Corn lacks gluten entirely but can be used to make flatbreads or mixed with wheat flour for a corn-flavored, gluten-based bread.

The Role of Sugars in Bread

While not a necessary ingredient in bread, sugars play several roles in the bread-making process. They provide food for the yeast, encouraging fermentation. Sugars also enhance the flavor of the bread, contribute to browning via the Maillard reaction, and help to tenderize the crumb.

Enriched Breads vs. Lean Breads

Breads can be categorized into two broad categories based on their ingredients: enriched breads and lean breads. Lean breads are made with the basic ingredients of flour, water, yeast, and salt, while enriched breads include additional ingredients such as milk, butter, eggs, and sugar.

Enriched breads tend to be softer, richer, and have a longer shelf-life than lean breads, but each has its unique appeal and uses. As you explore bread-baking, you'll discover which types you prefer to bake and consume.

The Concept of Hydration in Bread Making

One term you'll frequently encounter in bread-making circles is "hydration," which refers to the amount of water in a bread recipe in relation to the amount of flour. This is often expressed as a percentage. For instance, a dough with 500 grams of flour and 350 grams of water would have a hydration level of 70%.

The hydration level significantly impacts the dough's handling and the final bread's texture. Lower hydration doughs (50–60%) are generally easier to handle and yield a firmer, more structured crumb, while higher hydration doughs (70% and above) can be more challenging to work with but produce bread with an open, airy crumb and a lovely, thin crust.

The Importance of Temperature in Bread-Making

Temperature plays a significant role in bread-making. Yeast activity is highly dependent on temperature; warmer temperatures speed up fermentation, while cooler temperatures slow it down. This can be used to your advantage in controlling the fermentation process. For instance, dough can be refrigerated for a process known as cold fermentation, which slows down yeast activity, allowing flavors to develop more fully.

Temperature is also crucial during baking. Most bread is baked at high temperatures (around 425–475°F or 220–245°C) to encourage a good oven spring and a nice, golden crust. However, the optimal baking temperature can vary depending on the type of bread.

Experimenting with Add-Ins

Once you're comfortable with the basics of bread-making, you can start to experiment with add-ins. Seeds, nuts, dried fruits, herbs, spices, and even cheeses can be added to your dough to create an endless variety of flavors and textures.

Bread and Sourdough Mastery

When adding ingredients to your dough, it's essential to consider their impact on the overall bread-making process. For example, ingredients like seeds and whole grains can absorb water, potentially affecting the dough's hydration. Others, like cheese, could impact the baking process due to their melting point and moisture content.

Scoring: More Than Just Decoration

Scoring, or slashing the top of the loaf with a sharp blade or a baker's lame right before baking, serves two primary purposes: it allows the bread to expand properly during baking, and it gives the bread its distinctive appearance.

The way you score your bread can affect how it expands, or "blooms," in the oven. A simple central slash will give the loaf a more uniform shape, while a pattern of slashes can create a more rustic appearance. Whatever way you decide to score your bread, the key is to make decisive, swift cuts.

As you can see, bread-making is a complex and rewarding journey, not a destination. The most important thing is to enjoy the process, from the tactile pleasure of kneading the dough to enjoying the aroma of fresh bread baking in the oven. And remember, every loaf you bake, whether perfect or imperfect, is a step on your path to mastering the art of bread-making.

Now that we've covered the basic understanding of bread-making, we're ready to delve into the world of sourdough baking. This natural, time-honored process of leavening bread uses a live fermented culture of flour and water, resulting in a unique and delicious loaf of bread.

Chapter 2

Baker's Alchemy: The Chemistry of Bread

Understanding the chemistry of bread-making allows a baker to move from purely following recipes to actually creating them! The art of baking bread, one of humanity's most ancient forms of sustenance, is a fascinating alchemical process of transforming simple ingredients—flour, water, yeast, and salt—into something wholesome and delicious. This process is far from simple, driven by complex biochemistry, thermodynamics, and even physics. By delving into the science behind this magic, one can master the art of baking bread.

The Flour Power: Unleashing the Potential of Gluten

Every great bread begins with flour, and it's in this powdery substance that we find the proteins, glutenin and gliadin. When mixed with water and subjected to mechanical force (like kneading), these proteins hydrate and intertwine, creating a complex network we know as gluten.

Gluten is the backbone of our bread, providing the necessary structure and elasticity. It's responsible for trapping the gases produced by yeast or sourdough during the fermentation process, which, in turn, causes the dough to rise. The more the dough is worked, the stronger this network becomes, which can influence the bread's final texture and crumb structure.

Water: The Unsung Hero of Bread-Making

The role of water in bread making extends beyond merely hydrating the flour. It serves multiple functions—it helps form the gluten matrix, dissolves yeast, salt, and sugars, and plays a pivotal role in controlling the dough's temperature.

Bread and Sourdough Mastery

The amount of water used in relation to flour, known as dough's hydration, significantly affects the bread's characteristics. High hydration doughs, for instance, yield bread with an open, irregular crumb structure, while lower hydration results in a denser, more regular crumb. Understanding how hydration impacts dough behavior is key to manipulating it to achieve desired results.

Salt: Enhancer of Flavor and Function

While seemingly a minor ingredient, salt has a profound effect on bread. It enhances the flavor, strengthens the gluten network, controls yeast activity, and improves crust color. Without salt, bread can taste flat and dull. Additionally, it tightens the gluten structure, making it less sticky and easier to work with, and slows down fermentation, providing better flavor development.

The Magic of Yeast: The Process of Fermentation

Yeast is a living organism, and when given the right environment—a moist mixture of flour and water with a pinch of sugar—it begins to consume the sugars present in the flour. As yeast metabolizes these sugars, it produces carbon dioxide gas and ethanol as by-products, a process known as fermentation.

The gluten network traps this carbon dioxide, causing the dough to rise and gain volume. This is called leavening. The ethanol produced contributes to the bread's unique aroma and flavor.

The Maillard Reaction and Caramelization: Crust Formation and Coloring

Bread's delightful golden-brown crust is a result of two primary chemical reactions: the Maillard reaction and caramelization. The Maillard reaction occurs when the sugars and amino acids on the dough's surface react under high heat, producing hundreds of flavor compounds and that distinct bready aroma.

Simultaneously, caramelization, the process by which sugars break down and oxidize when subjected to high heat, gives the crust its appealing brown color and a slightly sweet, complex flavor. Both these processes contribute immensely to the flavor profile and visual appeal of the final loaf.

Starch Gelatinization: Crumb Formation and Texture

This process, known as starch gelatinization, continues as the water turns into steam, causing the dough to expand and rise rapidly in the oven, a phenomenon referred to as "oven spring". As the temperature inside the bread reaches the boiling point of water, the starches solidify, giving the crumb its structure. The proteins also coagulate at this stage, solidifying into the familiar bread texture.

Enzymes at Work: Amylase and Protease

Enzymes present in the flour and added yeast also play a critical role in bread-baking. Two enzymes—amylase and protease—have a particularly significant impact.

Amylase breaks down starches in the flour into simpler sugars. Yeast can then ferment these sugars, producing carbon dioxide gas that leavens the bread. Amylase activity also contributes to the Maillard reaction and caramelization during baking, as these processes require sugars.

Protease, on the other hand, breaks down proteins. While this can weaken the gluten network, a small amount of protease activity is beneficial as it can help make the dough more extensible and easier to shape.

The Effect of Temperature and Time

Temperature and time are two variables that a baker always needs to control. The rate at which yeast ferments sugars into carbon dioxide and ethanol is highly dependent on the dough's temperature. As we have noted earlier, generally, warmer temperatures speed up the fermentation, while cooler ones slow it down.

The time taken for each stage of bread-making, from mixing to proofing to baking, also has a significant impact on the final loaf. For instance, longer fermentation times can lead to more complex flavors in the bread but may also result in over-proofing if not monitored closely.

Bread and Sourdough Mastery

Understanding Oven Spring and Scoring

When the shaped dough first enters the oven, it rapidly expands due to the heat, resulting in what we bakers call "oven spring". This is a crucial phase where the bread gains much of its final volume. Scoring or slashing the loaf just before baking allows this rapid expansion to occur without tearing the bread's surface. It also gives the baker some control over how and where the bread will expand, influencing the final loaf's appearance.

The Role of Fats and Sweeteners

While not always used in traditional bread recipes, the addition of fats and sweeteners can significantly alter the bread's texture and flavor. Fats can enrich the dough, making it softer and extending the bread's shelf-life. They achieve this by coating some of the protein molecules, preventing them from forming as much gluten, resulting in a more tender crumb.

Sweeteners, apart from adding flavor, provide additional food for yeast, enhance browning through caramelization, and can help retain moisture in the bread, keeping it fresher for longer.

Practical Experimentation: The Hands-On Approach

Now that we've explored the theory, it's time to put this knowledge into practice. Baking is a highly practical craft, and nothing can substitute for hands-on experience. Try making adjustments in your next baking session—change the hydration, knead a little more or a little less, alter the proofing times—and observe how these changes affect the final product. Each loaf you bake is a science experiment unfolding before you, and your kitchen is your laboratory.

Troubleshooting Common Baking Issues

With an understanding of bread's underlying chemistry, you are well equipped to troubleshoot many common baking problems. Bread didn't rise enough? Maybe the yeast was old or the dough was too cold. The crust is too thick or dark? Perhaps the oven was too hot, or the bread was baked for too long. The crumb too dense? Possibly too much flour, insufficient kneading, or not enough proofing time.

The Subtleties of Sourdough
The chemistry behind sourdough bread is slightly different. Sourdough relies on a mixture of wild yeast and lactic acid bacteria, both present in the environment. The yeast functions similarly to commercial yeast, fermenting the sugars to produce carbon dioxide. The bacteria, on the other hand, consume the sugars to produce lactic acid, giving sourdough its characteristic tangy flavor. The interplay between yeast and bacteria, and how they influence sourdough's flavor and texture, is a fascinating area to explore, and we'll delve deeper into it in later chapters.

The Never-Ending Journey of Learning

Bread-making is a lifelong journey of learning and discovery. Even professional bakers with years of experience continuously experiment and learn, striving to perfect their craft. So, never be disheartened by bread that doesn't turn out as expected. Instead, view it as an opportunity to learn and improve.

The Art and Science of Bread-Baking

As we have seen, baking bread is a beautiful harmony of art and science. The science allows us to understand what's happening at each stage of the bread-making process, while the art allows us to apply this knowledge creatively, bringing our own personal touch and innovation to the craft. This delicate balance between science and art is what makes baking bread such a unique and rewarding culinary practice.

The Importance of Quality Ingredients

Just as in any culinary endeavor, the quality of the ingredients used in bread-baking can significantly affect the end product. Using high-quality, fresh ingredients can enhance the flavor, texture, and overall quality of your bread. This includes everything from the flour and yeast to the water and salt.

Experimenting with Different Flours

Different types of flour can bring different flavors and textures to your bread. While white wheat flour is most commonly used, experimenting with whole wheat, rye, spelt, and other grains can add interesting dimensions to your baking repertoire. Each type of flour has its own unique properties in terms of gluten content, flavor, and behavior, allowing for endless possibilities in bread-baking.

Pushing the Boundaries: Advanced Baking Techniques

As you become more comfortable with the basics of bread-baking and the science behind it, you can start exploring more advanced techniques. These can include longer fermentation periods, the use of pre-ferments or sourdough starters, complex shaping techniques, and more. These techniques, while requiring more skill and experience, can take your bread-baking to new heights, allowing you to create artisan-quality breads at home.

The Joy of Sharing Your Bread

One of the most rewarding aspects of bread-baking is the ability to share your creations with others. There is a certain joy and satisfaction in seeing the smiles on the faces of your loved ones as they enjoy a slice of fresh, homemade bread that you've created with your own hands. This sense of sharing and community is at the heart of bread-baking.

The Magic of Fermentation: A Closer Look

While we've so far touched upon fermentation, this natural process deserves the spotlight. Fermentation, driven by the yeast in your dough, is nothing short of magical. This biological process breathes life into the raw ingredients, transforming a simple mixture of flour and water into a living, bubbling entity. This transformation is so dramatic that it has its own name in baking lingo—the dough is said to be "alive"!

We'll delve deeper into the intricacies of fermentation in later chapters, especially when we discuss sourdough bread. However, at this point, it's important to understand that the rate of fermentation is crucial in determining the texture, size, and flavor of your bread. Understanding and controlling this process is a crucial skill in the baker's repertoire.

The Mystery of Gluten: The Key to Bread's Structure

Gluten, a complex matrix of proteins found in wheat, is another fascinating topic that deserves a closer look. Gluten's unique ability to form stretchy, elastic networks when combined with water is what gives bread its structure and texture. The complex interaction between glutenin and gliadin, the two primary components of gluten, is what allows dough to trap the gases produced by yeast, causing the bread to rise.

Baker's Percentage: Mastering the Math of Baking

In professional baking, recipes are often presented using "baker's percentages". This system expresses each ingredient's weight as a percentage of the total flour weight. This may seem confusing at first, but it's a powerful tool for scaling recipes up or down and understanding the relationships between different ingredients. A thorough understanding of baker's percentages can make you a more versatile and confident baker.

Hydration: The Key to Dough Consistency

As we have seen, in baking terms, hydration refers to the amount of water in a dough, expressed as a percentage of the total flour weight. The level of hydration in a dough dramatically affects the final product, influencing everything from the bread's texture to its crust. High hydration doughs, which contain a larger proportion of water, typically result in bread with an open crumb and a shiny, crispy crust. On the other hand, low hydration doughs tend to produce bread with a denser crumb and a softer crust.

The Impact of Salt: More Than Just Flavor

Salt plays a much larger role in bread baking than simply adding flavor. It strengthens the gluten network in the dough, slows down yeast fermentation, and aids in crust browning. Its impact on both the texture and flavor of the bread is so significant that forgetting to add salt can be disastrous!

Shaping and Scoring: The Final Touches

Once your dough has fermented and risen, shaping it into a beautiful loaf is an art in itself. The way you shape your dough can affect the final loaf's appearance, crumb structure, and even its flavor. Similarly, scoring, or making strategic cuts on the dough's surface before baking, can control how the bread expands in the oven, influencing its final shape and appearance. Mastering these techniques can truly elevate your baking skills.

The Love of Baking: An Art and a Science

We end this chapter by re-emphasizing the unique blend of science and art that is bread-baking. Each loaf of bread you bake is a testament to the miraculous transformation of simple ingredients under the influence of time, temperature, and the baker's touch. As you continue your journey into the world of baking, remember to appreciate the science, enjoy the process, and savor the delicious results.

From Dough to Bread: The Baking Process

The transformation that dough undergoes in the oven is yet another marvel of bread-baking. As the temperature increases, the water in the dough begins to vaporize, causing the bread to expand even further. This oven spring is responsible for a significant portion of the bread's final volume. Simultaneously, the heat causes the proteins and starches in the dough to set, forming the firm structure of the bread. Finally, the crust browns and develops flavor due to Maillard reactions and caramelization, the same chemical reactions that give a seared steak or a roasted coffee bean their appetizing colors and flavors.

Whole Grains and Other Flours

As we move forward, we'll also delve into the world of whole grains and other types of flour beyond white wheat. Each grain brings a different flavor, texture, and nutritional profile to the table, and learning to bake with a variety of grains can add depth and diversity to your baking repertoire. From the nutty flavors of whole wheat and rye to the delicate sweetness of oats and corn, there's a world of flavors waiting to be explored.

Temperature and Time: The Invisible Ingredients

Temperature and time, though often overlooked, are critical components of bread baking. From the temperature of your ingredients to the temperature of your kitchen and oven, each degree can make a difference in your final product. Similarly, time plays a critical role at every stage of the process, from mixing and fermenting to baking and cooling. Learning to control these variables and use them to your advantage is a vital part of mastering the art of bread baking.

Sourdough Baking: An Ancient Tradition

In later chapters, we'll delve deep into the world of sourdough baking, an ancient tradition that predates the use of commercial yeast. Sourdough bread relies on a fermented mixture of flour and water, known as a "starter", which acts as a natural leavening agent. Baking with sourdough is a labor of love that requires patience and skill, but the reward is bread with exceptional flavor, texture, and keeping quality.

Advanced Techniques: Taking Your Baking to the Next Level

As you continue to build your skills and understanding, you'll be ready to explore more advanced bread-baking techniques. From slow fermentation and autolyse to lamination and high-hydration doughs, these methods can help you achieve professional-quality results in your home kitchen. We'll explore these topics in detail, providing you with the knowledge and confidence to tackle these techniques.

Celebrating Bread: A Universal Food

Finally, let's take a moment to appreciate bread in its larger context. Bread is more than just a food item; it's a symbol of sustenance and community that transcends cultures and generations. From the baguettes of France to the naan of India, the tortillas of Mexico to the rye bread of Scandinavia, every culture has its unique take on this universal food. As you continue your journey into the world of bread-baking, I invite you to explore and celebrate this diversity.

As we wrap up this chapter, I hope you now have a deeper understanding and appreciation for the science and chemistry that underpin the art of bread-baking. With this knowledge in hand, you're well-equipped to take your baking skills to the next level. So put on your apron, roll up your sleeves, and let's explore our baking journey together. In the next chapter, we'll take a deep dive into the world of sourdough, exploring its unique process, challenges, and rewards. Stay tuned!

Alan Collins

Chapter 3

The Sourdough Starter: Beginning Your Bread Journey

The journey into sourdough baking is unlike any other. It's an adventure that calls for patience, curiosity, and a dash of scientific know-how. At the heart of this journey is the sourdough starter—a simple, fermented mixture of flour and water teeming with wild yeasts and beneficial bacteria. It's your personal pocket of leavening power, ready to raise doughs to new heights and imbue your bread with distinctive flavors and textures. This chapter aims to take you through the process of creating, maintaining, and using a sourdough starter from scratch.

The Magic of Wild Yeast

To understand the sourdough starter, we first need to comprehend the magic of wild yeast. Unlike commercial yeast, wild yeast is everywhere—in the air we breathe, on the grains of wheat we mill, and even on our hands. When given a conducive environment, these wild yeasts come to life, eagerly consuming the sugars in flour and producing carbon dioxide, alcohol, and a slew of flavorful compounds in return.

The Symbiotic Relationship: Yeast and Bacteria

In the world of sourdough, yeast doesn't work alone. A sourdough starter is a thriving microbial community, a symbiotic culture of wild yeasts and lactic acid bacteria. These bacteria feed on the byproducts of yeast fermentation, creating lactic and acetic acid. These acids give sourdough its distinctive tangy flavor while also creating an environment that helps keep harmful microbes at bay.

Creating Your Starter: The Beginning

Starting your sourdough starter is as simple as mixing flour and water in a jar. However, the simplicity of the ingredients belies the complexity of what's happening under the surface. As soon as you mix the flour and water, the yeasts and bacteria present in the flour and your environment get to work, slowly colonizing the mixture and starting the fermentation process.

Feeding and Maintenance

Once the initial mixture is set, the starter needs regular feeding to keep the yeast and bacteria happy and active. This involves adding fresh flour and water, which provide the microorganisms with a new source of food, allowing them to multiply and continue the fermentation process. The frequency and ratio of these feedings can affect the flavor and activity level of your starter, and part of the art of sourdough baking is learning to adjust these variables based on your specific conditions and preferences.

Watching and Waiting: Signs of Activity

The first few days of creating a sourdough starter are a test of patience. It might take several days before you see any signs of life in your starter. However, with each feeding, the microbial community in your starter is slowly growing and becoming more active. The first bubbles, a sign of yeast activity and gas production, are a cause for celebration—they're a clear indication that your starter is coming to life!

Troubleshooting Your Starter

Despite our best intentions, sometimes our sourdough starters might need a little troubleshooting. Perhaps the activity in your starter has slowed down, or maybe it's producing more liquid (hooch) than usual. Understanding the signs of a healthy and unhealthy starter and knowing how to troubleshoot common issues is an essential part of the sourdough journey.

The Power of Temperature

Temperature is a powerful variable in the world of sourdough. Yeast and bacteria activity are highly dependent on the surrounding temperature—a warmer environment can speed up fermentation, while a cooler one slows it down. This can be used to your advantage, allowing you to control the fermentation process by manipulating the temperature of your environment, your ingredients, or even your starter itself.

The Importance of Consistency

Consistency is key when it comes to maintaining a sourdough starter. The regular feeding of your starter keeps the population of yeast and bacteria at an optimal level. Not only does this ensure that your starter is ready to leaven bread at any given time, but it also influences the flavor of your final product. A well-fed and regularly refreshed starter will produce a more mildly flavored bread, while a neglected or "starving" starter will give a tangier loaf.

Flour Choices: Affecting Flavor and Activity

The type of flour you use to feed your starter can significantly influence its flavor and activity level. While a starter can be maintained on a wide range of flours, each brings something different to the table. For instance, whole grain flours are often richer in nutrients and wild yeasts, which can lead to a more active and flavorful starter. On the other hand, white flour can give you a milder flavor and a more predictable feeding schedule.

Understanding Hydration Levels

The hydration level of your starter, or the ratio of water to flour by weight, is another crucial variable in sourdough baking. A high-hydration starter (100% or more) will be wetter, ferment faster, and typically produce a milder flavor. A lower hydration starter (below 100%), on the other hand, will have a dough-like consistency, ferment slower, and produce a tangier flavor. Understanding and adjusting hydration levels can help you tailor your sourdough baking to your preferences.

Hooch: A Sign of Hunger

If you've ever noticed a layer of liquid on top of your starter, you've encountered "hooch." This alcoholic byproduct of yeast fermentation is a clear sign that your starter is hungry and needs feeding. Regular feeding of your starter can prevent hooch from forming and keep your starter at its optimal health.

The Refrigeration Trick: Slowing Things Down

One of the biggest challenges sourdough bakers can face is aligning the feeding schedule of a starter with the demands of daily life. Thankfully, there's a simple solution: your refrigerator. By storing your starter in the fridge, you can significantly slow down the fermentation process, allowing you to reduce the feeding frequency to once a week. This can be a game-changer for home bakers who want to enjoy sourdough baking without being tied to a daily feeding schedule.

Waking Up a Refrigerated Starter

When you're ready to bake, a refrigerated starter will need a little time to "wake up" and reach its full leavening potential. This usually involves one or two feedings at room temperature before you start mixing your dough. Understanding how to properly wake up your starter will ensure that it's ready to give its all in your next batch of bread.

Discard: The Unavoidable Byproduct

Feeding your starter inevitably leads to an excess of starter, often referred to as "discard." While it may seem wasteful to throw away this discard, it's an essential part of maintaining a healthy and vibrant starter. However, that doesn't mean discard can't be put to good use! There are countless recipes out there for sourdough discard, from pancakes and muffins to crackers and even cakes.

A Living Ingredient: The Unique Joys of Sourdough

The most extraordinary aspect of a sourdough starter is that it's a living entity. No two starters are precisely the same, and each will impart its unique character to your bread. Caring for a sourdough starter can be a rewarding journey that connects you to the ancient traditions of bread-baking and opens the door to a world of rich flavors and textures.

Scaling Up: Preparing for Baking

Bread and Sourdough Mastery

When you're ready to embark on the baking process, you will need more starter than you typically keep on hand. This is where "scaling up" comes in. A few days before you plan to bake, you can start adding more flour and water at each feeding, gradually increasing the volume of your starter. This not only provides you with the quantity needed for your baking endeavors but also ensures that your starter is at its peak activity when it's time to mix your dough.

Scaling up your starter involves increasing the ratio of flour and water in each feeding. For example, if you typically feed your starter with equal parts flour and water (100% hydration), you can increase it to a higher hydration, such as 150% or even 200%. This means adding more water to create a looser consistency, which promotes yeast activity and fermentation.

By gradually increasing the volume of your starter, you are essentially increasing the population of yeast and bacteria. This leads to a stronger, more active starter that can leaven your bread effectively. It's important to monitor the growth and activity of your starter during this process to ensure it is developing well and not becoming overly acidic.

Remember to adjust your feeding routine accordingly as you scale up your starter. You may need to feed it more frequently or increase the amount of flour and water at each feeding to accommodate the increased volume. The goal is to maintain a healthy and vibrant starter that is ready to perform its leavening magic in your bread.

Testing for Readiness: The Float Test

A crucial skill to learn in sourdough baking is knowing when your starter is ready to be used in a dough. One popular method to determine its readiness is the float test. By dropping a small spoonful of starter into a glass of water, you can assess its buoyancy.

To perform the float test, take a small amount of your fully fed starter and drop it gently into a glass of room temperature water. Observe whether the starter floats or sinks. If it floats and stays at the surface, it indicates that the starter is active and full of enough gases produced by the yeast. This means it is ready to leaven your bread. If it sinks, it may need more time to ferment or might require a fresh feeding before it is at its peak activity.

It's important to note that the float test is just one method to determine starter readiness. You can also rely on visual cues like the volume doubling after feeding, the presence of bubbles, and the aroma of the starter. Ultimately, experience and experimentation will help you understand the unique behavior of your particular starter.

Establishing a Feeding Routine

Creating a consistent feeding routine that fits into your lifestyle is vital to maintaining a healthy sourdough starter. Some bakers prefer a daily feeding, while others opt for a twice-a-day regimen. The frequency of feeding depends on various factors, such as the temperature of your kitchen, the type of flour used, and the maturity of your starter. A general rule of thumb is that a happy starter doubles in size within 4 to 8 hours of feeding.

To establish a feeding routine, it's helpful to observe the behavior of your starter over a few feeding cycles. Note how quickly it rises after feeding and how long it maintains its peak activity before deflating. This will give you an idea of its feeding frequency requirements.

Choose a feeding schedule that aligns with your daily routine and allows you to maintain a consistent cycle. For example, if you prefer a daily feeding, you can feed your starter at the same time each day, ensuring that it's always at its most active state when you need it for baking.

Consistency is key when it comes to feeding your starter. Aim to use the same type of flour and maintain a consistent hydration level throughout the feeding process. This helps establish a stable environment for the microorganisms in your starter, promoting their growth and activity.

During each feeding, discard a portion of your starter to prevent it from becoming too large. The discarded portion or "discard" can be used in various recipes like pancakes, waffles, or even as a flavor booster in bread doughs. By discarding and refreshing your starter, you maintain a manageable amount and ensure its vitality.

Exploring Different Grains

Bread and Sourdough Mastery

While most sourdough starters are made with wheat, there's a world of grains to explore in your sourdough journey. Rye, spelt, and even gluten-free grains like rice and millet can all be used to create unique starters. Each grain brings its flavor profile, fermentation speed, and nutritional benefits, offering endless possibilities for customizing your sourdough bread.

Rye is a popular choice for sourdough starters due to its high microbial activity and distinctive flavor. It often ferments more quickly than wheat, producing a tangy and robust starter. Spelt, an ancient grain, has a milder flavor and can be a great option for those who prefer a less tangy sourdough taste.

Experimenting with different grains can open up a world of flavors in your sourdough bread. You can use these alternative starters alone or in combination with wheat flour to create unique flavor profiles. Remember to adjust the feeding ratio and hydration levels based on the specific requirements of each grain to ensure a healthy and active starter.

As you explore different grains, keep in mind that some may require specific conditions or techniques to achieve optimal fermentation. Research and experimentation will guide you in adapting your feeding routine and understanding the unique characteristics of each grain.

Observing the Life Cycle of Your Starter

Observing and understanding the life cycle of your starter is a lesson in microbiology. It's a cycle that begins with the 'feeding'—the moment you add fresh flour and water. At this point, the yeasts and bacteria in your starter start consuming the new food, and the starter begins to rise.

As the yeasts ferment the sugars in the flour, they produce carbon dioxide gas, which gets trapped in the gluten network of the dough, causing it to expand. This is the "peak" of the cycle, where the starter has reached its maximum volume. It's also the perfect time to use the starter to leaven a dough.

After the peak, the starter begins to fall. The yeast has consumed most of the available food, and the gas production slows down, causing the starter to deflate. At this point, the starter will taste more sour, because the bacteria have had more time to produce acids.

Understanding this life cycle can give you more control over your baking process. For example, if you want a milder flavor, you can use the starter at its peak or even before it starts to fall. If you desire a more tangy flavor, you can use the starter when it's fully matured and has gone through the entire cycle.

Troubleshooting Common Starter Issues

Like any living organism, sourdough starters can encounter issues along the way. Understanding common problems and how to troubleshoot them is essential for maintaining a healthy starter. Here are some common issues you may encounter:

a. Sluggish Starter: If your starter is not rising or showing signs of activity after feeding, it may be sluggish. This could be due to factors such as low room temperature, insufficient food (flour), or the presence of unwanted bacteria. Try adjusting the feeding ratio, increasing the temperature, or refreshing the starter with a higher proportion of fresh flour and water.

b. Excessive Acidity: If your starter becomes overly acidic, it can result in a sour taste that is too intense. This can happen if the starter is left at room temperature for an extended period between feedings or if it's fed with a high proportion of whole grain flour. To reduce acidity, consider adjusting the feeding frequency or using a larger proportion of white flour in your feedings.

c. Foul Odor: A foul or unpleasant odor from your starter may indicate the presence of undesirable bacteria or yeast. This can happen if the starter is contaminated or not fed frequently enough. In such cases, it's recommended to discard a portion of the starter and refresh it with fresh flour and water. If the problem persists, you may need to start a new starter from scratch.

d. Mold Growth: While rare, mold growth can occur on the surface of your starter, especially if it's left uncovered or in a humid environment. If you notice mold, it's crucial to discard the entire starter and thoroughly clean the container. Starting anew with a clean and sanitized container is essential to prevent mold recurrence.

Bread and Sourdough Mastery

Remember that troubleshooting is part of the sourdough journey. Each issue you encounter is an opportunity to learn and refine your understanding of the fermentation process. Don't be discouraged if you face challenges along the way; instead, embrace them as valuable lessons.

Adapting Your Starter to Your Needs

As you become more comfortable with your starter, you can adapt it to suit your baking preferences. Here are a few ways to customize your starter:

a. Adjusting Hydration: The hydration level of your starter affects its consistency and fermentation activity. If you prefer a more liquid starter, increase the water-to-flour ratio (higher hydration). For a firmer starter, decrease the water content (lower hydration). Experiment with different hydration levels to find what works best for your baking style.

b. Altering Feeding Ratios: The ratio of flour to water in your feedings can also impact the flavor and activity of your starter. Increasing the flour portion can lead to a milder flavor, while more water can contribute to a tangier taste. Play around with different ratios to discover the flavor profile that appeals to you.

c. Introducing Specialty Flours: Beyond the standard white and whole wheat flours, you can experiment with specialty flours like rye, spelt, or ancient grains. These flours bring unique flavors and characteristics to your starter, allowing you to create bread with distinct taste profiles.

d. Incorporating Other Ingredients: While flour and water are the primary ingredients for a sourdough starter, you can introduce other elements to add depth and complexity. Some bakers add small amounts of fruits, honey, or yogurt to enhance flavor and jump-start fermentation. However, be mindful of the quantities and their potential impact on the balance of microorganisms in your starter.

By adapting your starter to your needs, you can create bread that aligns with your preferences and baking goals. The beauty of sourdough lies in its flexibility and the endless possibilities for customization.

The Joy of Sharing and Preserving Your Starter

As your sourdough journey progresses, you may find yourself with an abundance of starter. This presents an opportunity to share the joy of baking with others. Sharing your starter with friends, family, or fellow baking enthusiasts not only fosters a sense of community but also ensures the longevity of the sourdough tradition.

When sharing your starter, provide detailed instructions on how to care for it, including feeding schedules and temperatures. This helps ensure that the recipient can maintain the starter's vitality and continue to bake with it. Sharing starter is a beautiful way to pass on the knowledge and enthusiasm for sourdough baking.

If you need to take a break from baking or have excess starter that you can't give away, there are options for preserving it. You can dehydrate a portion of your starter by spreading it thinly on parchment paper and allowing it to dry completely. Once dry, store it in an airtight container at room temperature. When you're ready to revive it, simply rehydrate it with water and flour.

Alternatively, you can store a small amount of your starter in the refrigerator for a longer period. Feed it regularly (about once a week) to maintain its activity. When you're ready to bake again, gradually increase the feeding frequency and volume to revive it fully.

Preserving your starter ensures that you can always return to your sourdough journey, even after an extended break. It's a way to maintain the connection with this living culture and the art of sourdough baking.

Conclusion

In this chapter, we explored the intricacies of starting and maintaining a sourdough starter. We discussed scaling up your starter for baking, testing its readiness, establishing a feeding routine, exploring different grains, observing its life cycle, troubleshooting common issues, and adapting it to your needs. We also touched on the joy of sharing and preserving your starter.

Now that you have a solid foundation in sourdough starters, you're ready to move forward on your bread-baking journey. In the upcoming chapters, we will dive into the art of fermenting sourdough bread dough, shaping and scoring your loaves, and the final stages of baking. Get ready to unlock the full potential of your starter and experience the satisfaction of creating delicious homemade sourdough bread.

Chapter 4

Mastering the Basic Loaf: Your First Artisanal Bread

Congratulations on reaching the point where you're ready to bake your first loaf of artisanal bread! This chapter will guide you through the process of creating a classic, basic loaf using your sourdough starter. We'll cover everything from mixing the dough to baking it to perfection. Get ready to experience the satisfaction of creating a beautiful, flavorful loaf of bread from scratch.

Gathering Your Ingredients

Before you begin, make sure you have all your ingredients ready. For a basic loaf, you'll need:

Flour: Use a high-quality bread flour or a combination of bread flour and whole wheat flour for added flavor and texture.

Water: Filtered or spring water is ideal, as chlorine in tap water can affect the fermentation process.

Sourdough Starter: Ensure your starter is fully activated and at its peak activity.

Salt: Use fine sea salt or kosher salt to enhance the flavor of the bread.

Having everything prepared and within reach will help streamline the baking process.

Mixing the Dough

Mixing the dough is the first step in creating your artisanal bread. Here's a step-by-step process:

In a large mixing bowl, combine the flour, water, and sourdough starter. Use your hands or a dough scraper to incorporate the ingredients until a shaggy dough forms.

Let the dough rest for 20–30 minutes. This resting period, known as autolyse, allows the flour to fully hydrate and the gluten to begin developing.

After the autolyse, sprinkle the salt over the dough and knead it for about 10–15 minutes. You can use the stretch and fold method or traditional kneading techniques. The goal is to develop a smooth, elastic dough.

Bulk Fermentation

Once the dough is mixed and kneaded, it's time for bulk fermentation. This is the crucial stage where the yeast and bacteria in your sourdough starter work their magic, creating flavor and texture in the dough. Here's what you need to do:

Place the dough in a lightly oiled bowl, cover it with a kitchen towel or plastic wrap, and let it rest at room temperature for several hours. The exact duration will depend on various factors, including the temperature of your kitchen and the activity of your starter. Typically, bulk fermentation lasts anywhere from 4 to 8 hours.

During bulk fermentation, perform a series of gentle folds every 30 minutes for the first 2–3 hours. This helps strengthen the dough and distribute the fermentation byproducts evenly.

Shaping the Loaf

After the bulk fermentation, it's time to shape your dough into a loaf. Follow these steps:

Gently transfer the dough onto a lightly floured surface. Handle the dough with care to preserve the air bubbles created during fermentation.

Fold the dough over itself to create tension on the surface. You can use the letter fold or envelope fold method.

Flip the dough over and shape it into a tight, round ball by rotating it on the work surface.

Place the shaped dough into a well-floured proofing basket or a lined bowl, seam-side up.

Final Proofing

During the final proofing, the shaped loaf undergoes its last rise before baking. Here's what to do:

Cover the proofing basket or bowl with a kitchen towel and let the dough proof at room temperature for 1 to 2 hours. The time will vary depending on the ambient temperature and the activity of your starter. The dough should increase in volume and show signs of being "alive."

To check if the loaf is ready for baking, perform the "poke test." Gently press your fingertip into the dough. If it slowly springs back, the loaf is properly proofed. If the indentation remains, it needs more time for proofing.

Preparing for Baking

As your loaf is nearing the end of its final proof, it's time to preheat your oven and prepare the baking environment. Here's what you need to do:

Preheat your oven to a high temperature, usually around 450°F (230°C), for at least 30 minutes. Place a baking stone or a baking sheet inside the oven to heat up.

If you have a Dutch oven or a baking cloche, preheat it along with the oven. These enclosed containers help create a steamy environment that promotes oven spring and crust development.

Scoring the Loaf and Baking

Scoring the loaf is an essential step that allows the bread to expand properly during baking and creates a beautiful, artisanal appearance. Here's how to do it:

Carefully remove the proofed loaf from the basket or bowl onto a piece of parchment paper.

Using a sharp blade or a bread lame, make shallow, diagonal cuts or a pattern of your choice on the surface of the dough. This helps control the expansion and directs the oven spring.

Baking Your Loaf

Now that your loaf is scored and ready, it's time to bake it to golden perfection. Follow these steps:

Carefully transfer the parchment paper with the loaf onto the preheated baking stone or baking sheet in the oven. If using a Dutch oven or baking cloche, place the loaf inside the preheated container.

If you have a spray bottle filled with water, lightly mist the inside of the oven to create steam. This steam helps create a beautiful crust and promotes oven spring.

Close the oven door and reduce the temperature to around 400°F (200°C). The initial high temperature and steam help create a burst of oven spring.

Bake the loaf for about 20–25 minutes, then rotate it for even browning. Continue baking for another 20–25 minutes or until the loaf is deeply golden brown and sounds hollow when tapped on the bottom.

Once baked, remove the loaf from the oven and transfer it to a wire rack to cool completely before slicing. Allow the loaf to cool for at least an hour to ensure the crumb sets properly.

The Art of Slicing and Enjoying

Now comes the exciting part—slicing your freshly baked loaf and savoring the fruits of your labor! Here are a few tips for slicing and enjoying your artisanal bread:

Use a serrated bread knife or a sharp, non-serrated knife with a thin blade to slice through the crust without squishing the crumb.

To achieve even slices, start by cutting off the ends of the loaf, then proceed with gentle, steady motions to slice the desired thickness.

Admire the open crumb, the texture, and the aroma as you slice into your bread. Take a moment to appreciate the unique characteristics that make artisanal bread so special.

Enjoy your bread as it is or accompany it with butter, jams, spreads, or your favorite toppings. The possibilities are endless!

Troubleshooting and Refining

Your first attempt at baking artisanal bread may not be perfect, and that's okay! Baking is a skill that improves with practice. Here are some common troubleshooting tips and areas to refine as you continue your bread-baking journey:

Crust Color and Texture: If your crust is too pale or lacks a deep, golden color, you can try increasing the baking time or adjusting the oven temperature. To achieve a crisp crust, you can bake the loaf directly on the baking stone or remove the parchment paper during the last few minutes of baking.

Oven Spring: If your loaf doesn't achieve the desired oven spring or doesn't rise as much as expected, it could be due to various factors such as under-proofing, weak starter, or inadequate steam in the oven. Experiment with longer proofing times, refreshing your starter, and creating more steam in the oven to enhance oven spring.

Crumb Structure: The crumb of your bread refers to the interior texture. A well-developed gluten structure and proper fermentation contribute to an open and airy crumb. If your crumb is too dense, you may need to adjust your kneading technique, fermentation time, or hydration level of the dough.

Remember, every loaf you bake is an opportunity to learn and refine your techniques. Embrace the journey and enjoy the process of continuous improvement.

Flavor Variations: Adding Herbs, Seeds, and Spices

Once you have mastered the basic loaf, you can vary its flavor by incorporating herbs, seeds, and spices. These additions not only enhance the taste but also add visual interest and texture to your bread. Here are a few ideas to get you started:

a. Herbs: Fresh or dried herbs can infuse your bread with delightful aromas and flavors. Popular choices include rosemary, thyme, basil, dill, or oregano. Simply chop the herbs finely and incorporate them into the dough during the mixing process. Experiment with different combinations to find your favorite herb-infused bread.

b. Seeds: Adding seeds to your bread can provide a crunchy texture and a nutty flavor. Some common options include sesame seeds, poppy seeds, sunflower seeds, or flaxseeds. Mix the seeds into the dough or sprinkle them on top before baking for a decorative touch. Toasting the seeds before adding them to the dough can enhance their flavor even more.

c. Spices: Spices can lend a warm and aromatic quality to your bread. Cinnamon, nutmeg, cardamom, or even savory spices like cumin or turmeric can transform a basic loaf into something extraordinary. Add the spices to the dough during the mixing process, ensuring they are evenly distributed.

Remember to adjust the quantities of herbs, seeds, and spices to your personal preference. Start with smaller amounts and gradually increase until you achieve the desired flavor intensity.

Creating Artisanal Shapes: Boules, Batards, and Baguettes

While the basic loaf is a classic shape, exploring different shapes can add visual appeal to your artisanal bread. Here are a few common shapes to experiment with:

a. Boule: A boule is a round or slightly flattened shape, resembling a ball. To create a boule, shape the dough into a tight round ball and place it into a well-floured proofing basket or a bowl for the final proofing.

b. Batard: A batard is an elongated oval shape, similar to a football. After shaping the dough into a round boule, gently elongate it by folding the sides inward and sealing the seam at the bottom. Place the shaped batard on a well-floured surface or a baking sheet for the final proofing.

c. Baguette: The baguette is a long, slender loaf with a crisp crust and a chewy interior. To shape a baguette, divide the dough into smaller portions and roll each portion into a long, thin cylinder. Place the shaped baguettes on a floured couche (unbleached canvas cloth) or a baguette pan for the final proofing.

Experiment with different shapes to add variety and character to your bread collection. Remember to practice shaping techniques to achieve consistent and professional-looking results.

Advanced Techniques: Scoring and Decorative Patterns

Scoring is the process of making shallow cuts on the surface of the bread before baking. It not only adds an aesthetic element but also controls the expansion of the dough during baking. Here are some scoring techniques and decorative patterns you can try:

a. Single Slash: Make a single, diagonal slash across the top of the loaf. This simple yet elegant pattern allows the loaf to expand evenly.

b. Cross Slash: Create a cross-shaped pattern by making two intersecting diagonal cuts on the surface of the dough. This pattern adds a touch of sophistication to your bread.

c. Grid Pattern: Score a grid-like pattern by making perpendicular slashes on the surface of the dough. This creates a visually appealing design and allows the bread to expand in multiple directions.

d. Leaf or Wheat Pattern: Score the surface of the dough to resemble leaves or wheat stalks. This decorative pattern adds a rustic charm to your bread.

Remember to use a sharp blade or a bread lame for clean and precise scoring. Practice different patterns and experiment with your own unique designs to make your bread truly artistic.

Mastering Sourdough Enrichments: Filled and Swirled Breads

Sourdough enrichments refer to breads that incorporate additional ingredients like nuts, dried fruits, or chocolate. These additions not only enhance the flavor but also create a delightful texture in your bread. Here are a few sourdough enrichment ideas to try:

a. Walnut Raisin Bread: Add toasted walnuts and plump raisins to your dough. The combination of crunchy nuts and chewy fruits creates a delightful contrast.

b. Cinnamon Swirl Bread: Roll out the dough into a rectangle, spread a layer of cinnamon sugar, and roll it up tightly. This creates a beautiful swirl of cinnamon throughout the bread.

c. Chocolate Cherry Bread: Incorporate dark chocolate chunks and dried cherries into the dough. The rich chocolate and tart cherries create a decadent treat.

Experiment with different combinations and proportions of enrichments to create your own unique flavor profiles. Adjust the hydration level of the dough accordingly to accommodate the added ingredients.

Gluten-Free Sourdough Baking: Exploring Alternative Grains

If you follow a gluten-free diet, you can still enjoy the benefits of sourdough baking. There are various alternative grains that can be used to create gluten-free sourdough bread. Here are a few options:

a. Brown Rice Flour: Brown rice flour can be used as the main ingredient in gluten-free sourdough bread. It creates a mild and slightly nutty flavor.

b. Buckwheat Flour: Despite its name, buckwheat is not related to wheat and is naturally gluten-free. It adds a rich, earthy flavor to your bread.

c. Quinoa Flour: Quinoa flour is packed with nutrients and creates a light and fluffy texture in gluten-free bread. It has a slightly nutty and sweet flavor.

When working with alternative grains, it's essential to adjust the hydration level and fermentation times to achieve the best results. Gluten-free baking often requires a different approach, so be prepared for some experimentation and adjustments to your techniques.

Troubleshooting and Refining Techniques

As you embark on your bread-baking journey, it's essential to familiarize yourself with common troubleshooting issues and refining techniques to improve your bread-making skills. Here are some tips to help you troubleshoot and refine your techniques:

a. Dense Bread: If your bread turns out dense, this could be due to several factors. One possibility is insufficient fermentation time. Ensure that your dough has ample time to rise and develop gluten. Additionally, check the hydration level of your dough. If it's too dry, the bread may not have enough moisture to create a light and airy crumb. Experiment with adjusting the hydration and fermentation time to achieve a better texture.

b. Overproofed Bread: Overproofing occurs when the dough is left to rise for too long, resulting in a collapsed or flat loaf. To avoid overproofing, closely monitor the dough during the final proofing stage. Look for visual cues, such as a slight jiggle in the dough when gently tapped. If the dough feels overly soft or deflates easily, it may be overproofed. Adjust the proofing time accordingly to achieve optimal results.

c. Uneven Rise: If your bread has an uneven rise, with one side higher than the other, it may be due to improper shaping or uneven tension in the dough. When shaping your loaf, make sure to create a tight, even surface. Pay attention to the tension throughout the shaping process, ensuring that the dough is evenly distributed. Practice shaping techniques and strive for consistency to achieve a uniform rise.

d. Pale Crust: If your bread has a pale crust instead of a golden-brown color, it may be a result of insufficient oven temperature or baking time. Ensure that your oven is preheated to the recommended temperature before placing the dough inside. If necessary, increase the baking time slightly to achieve a desirable crust color. Additionally, consider using a baking stone or placing the dough directly on the oven rack to promote better heat distribution.

e. Soggy or Thick Crust: A soggy or thick crust can occur when the bread has excess moisture during baking or when steam is trapped inside the loaf. To achieve a crisp crust, allow steam to escape by leaving a small opening in the oven during the last few minutes of baking. If you prefer a softer crust, wrap the loaf in a clean kitchen towel while it cools to retain some moisture.

f. Adjusting Hydration: The hydration level of your dough plays a crucial role in achieving the desired texture and crumb structure. Experiment with adjusting the hydration by adding small increments of water or flour to achieve the desired consistency. Keep in mind that different flours may require varying hydration levels, so be open to adapting the recipe based on the flour you are using.

By addressing these troubleshooting areas and refining your techniques, you'll gradually develop a deeper understanding of the bread-making process and improve the quality of your loaves.

Experimentation and Personalization

Baking bread is an art that allows for endless creativity and personalization. As you continue your journey, don't be afraid to experiment with different ingredients, techniques, and flavors. Here are a few ways to personalize your bread:

a. Custom Flour Blends: Explore different types of flour to create unique flavor profiles. Experiment with whole wheat, rye, spelt, or ancient grains to add depth and complexity to your bread.

b. Incorporating Mix-Ins: Add your favorite mix-ins to the dough, such as chopped nuts, dried fruits, grated cheese, or olives. These additions can introduce new textures and flavors to your bread.

c. Artistic Scoring: Practice your scoring techniques and create beautiful patterns on the surface of your bread. Use your imagination to come up with unique designs that reflect your personal style.

d. Customizing Proofing Baskets: Invest in different types of proofing baskets, also known as bannetons, to shape your loaves. They come in various shapes and sizes, allowing you to experiment with different loaf shapes and create stunning visuals.

e. Exploring Regional Breads: Dive into the world of regional breads and learn about the unique techniques and flavors associated with different cultures. Challenge yourself to recreate these specialty breads in your own kitchen.

Remember, the joy of bread-baking lies not only in eating the final product but also in the process of making it. Embrace the opportunity to be creative, take risks, and make each loaf a unique expression of your passion for baking.

The Joy of Sharing: Bread as a Gift

One of the most rewarding aspects of baking bread is the opportunity to share your creations with others. Whether it's a special occasion, a gathering with loved ones, or simply a gesture of kindness, giving homemade bread as a gift is a wonderful way to spread joy. Here are some ideas for sharing your artisanal bread:

a. Gift Baskets: Create beautiful bread gift baskets by pairing your freshly baked loaves with complementary items. Include spreads like flavored butter, fruit preserves, or artisanal cheeses. Add a handwritten recipe card or a personalized note to make the gift even more special.

b. Dinner Parties: If you're invited to a dinner party or gathering, bring a freshly baked loaf of bread as a hostess gift. Not only will it show your appreciation, but it will also serve as a delightful addition to the meal.

c. Community Events: Consider participating in local food fairs, farmers' markets, or charity events. Share your artisanal bread with the community and engage in conversations about your passion for baking. It's a great way to connect with others who appreciate homemade goodness.

d. Random Acts of Kindness: Surprise a neighbor, a friend, or a coworker with a homemade loaf of bread. Leave it at their doorstep with a heartfelt note, expressing your appreciation or simply spreading some love.

Remember, the act of giving bread is as gratifying as the act of baking it. It creates a sense of connection, fosters goodwill, and brings smiles to the faces of those who receive your delicious creations.

Embracing the Journey

As you continue to master the basic loaf and explore the world of artisanal bread, it's important to remember that bread-baking is a journey, not a destination. It's a craft that requires practice, patience, and a genuine love for the process. Embrace the ups and downs, the successes and failures, and cherish every moment spent kneading, shaping, and baking.

Allow yourself to be inspired by the endless possibilities that bread-baking offers. Experiment with new flavors, techniques, and shapes. Learn from others in the bread-baking community, whether it's through books, online resources, or joining local baking groups. Engage in conversations, share your experiences, and celebrate the joy of baking bread.

By immersing yourself in the art of bread making, you will not only refine your skills but also nourish your soul. Each loaf you create becomes a testament to your dedication and passion for the craft. So, keep learning, keep exploring, and keep sharing the magic of homemade bread with the world.

Conclusion

In this chapter, you have embarked on the journey of mastering the basic loaf, expanding your skills, and discovering the joy of sharing homemade bread. You have learned about flavor variations, shaping techniques, troubleshooting, and the ways of gifting bread. By applying these principles, you are well on your way to becoming a confident and skilled artisanal bread baker.

Chapter 5

Embracing the Wild: An Introduction to Sourdough

Sourdough bread has a rich history that spans thousands of years. It is a true testament to the art of fermentation and the symbiotic relationship between wild yeast and bacteria. In this chapter, we will delve into the fascinating world of sourdough, exploring its origins, the science behind it, and the process of creating your own sourdough starter. Get ready to embark on a journey of tangy, flavorful bread that showcases the magic of natural fermentation.

The Origins of Sourdough

Sourdough bread has ancient origins, dating back to ancient Egypt and Mesopotamia. Before commercial yeast became widely available, people relied on wild yeast and lactobacilli present in the environment to leaven their bread. These naturally occurring microorganisms, particularly lactobacilli, give sourdough its distinct tangy flavor and characteristic texture.

The name "sourdough" is derived from the sour taste that develops during the fermentation process. Over time, sourdough bread has become deeply rooted in various cultures, each with its own unique techniques and flavors.

The Science of Sourdough

To understand the science behind sourdough, we need to explore the two key microorganisms involved: wild yeast and lactobacilli.

Bread and Sourdough Mastery

a. Wild Yeast: Wild yeast refers to the naturally occurring yeasts present in the environment. They are responsible for fermentation, converting sugars into carbon dioxide gas and alcohol. Wild yeast is what gives sourdough bread its rise.

b. Lactobacilli: Lactobacilli are a group of beneficial bacteria that produce lactic acid through fermentation. They thrive in the acidic environment created during sourdough fermentation. Lactic acid contributes to the tangy flavor, helps preserve the bread, and adds depth to the crumb structure.

The symbiotic relationship between wild yeast and lactobacilli is what sets sourdough apart from other types of bread. The yeast provides leavening, while the bacteria produce the distinctive sour taste and contribute to the bread's overall texture and keeping qualities.

Creating Your Sourdough Starter

A sourdough starter is the heart and soul of sourdough bread-baking. It is a fermented mixture of flour and water that captures wild yeast and lactobacilli from the environment. Establishing a healthy and active sourdough starter is the first step towards baking flavorful sourdough bread. Here's a step-by-step guide to creating your own sourdough starter:

a. Day 1: Combine equal parts of flour and water in a glass jar or container. Stir well until fully combined, ensuring no dry flour remains. Cover the jar loosely with a clean kitchen towel and let it sit at room temperature (around 70°F or 21°C) for 24 hours.

b. Day 2: Discard half of the starter and add equal amounts of flour and water (by weight) to the remaining starter. Mix well and cover loosely. Let it sit for another 24 hours.

c. Day 3: Repeat the same process of discarding half of the starter and feeding it with equal amounts of flour and water. By this stage, you may start to notice some activity in your starter, such as bubbles forming and a slightly sour smell.

d. Day 4 and Beyond: Continue discarding and feeding your starter once or twice a day, maintaining equal ratios of flour and water. As the fermentation progresses, your starter will become more active and develop a stronger sour smell. It is important to maintain regular feeding to keep the yeast and bacteria healthy and active.

It can take anywhere from 5 to 10 days for your starter to mature, depending on environmental factors and the specific microorganisms present in your location. Patience is key during this process. Once your starter is active, you are ready to bake with it.

Feeding and Maintaining Your Sourdough Starter

Once your sourdough starter is established, it requires regular feeding to keep it active and healthy. Here are some guidelines for feeding and maintaining your sourdough starter:

a. Feeding Schedule: Most bakers feed their starter once or twice a day, depending on their baking frequency. However, the feeding schedule can be adjusted to suit your lifestyle. If you're not baking regularly, you can refrigerate your starter and feed it once a week to maintain its vitality.

b. Discarding: When feeding your starter, it's important to discard a portion of the existing starter before refreshing it. Discarding helps control the acidity level and prevents the starter from becoming too acidic. A general rule of thumb is to discard at least half of the starter before feeding.

c. Feeding Ratios: The feeding ratios refer to the proportion of flour and water used to refresh your starter. A common ratio is equal amounts of flour and water (1:1), by weight. However, some bakers prefer a stiffer consistency and use a higher ratio of flour to water (e.g., 1:0.75).

d. Consistency and Temperature: The consistency of your starter can vary depending on your preference and the recipe you're following. A thicker starter (with less hydration) tends to ferment more slowly, while a looser starter (with higher hydration) ferments more quickly. Additionally, the temperature at which you maintain your starter affects the fermentation rate. Warmer temperatures accelerate fermentation, while cooler temperatures slow it down.

By understanding the feeding process and adapting it to your schedule and preferences, you can maintain a vibrant and active sourdough starter for years to come.

Bread and Sourdough Mastery

Fermentation and Dough Development

Once you have a lively sourdough starter, you can start using it to make bread dough. Fermentation is a crucial step in sourdough bread-making, as it allows the wild yeast and lactobacilli to work their magic and develop complex flavors. Here's a general overview of the fermentation process:

a. Autolyse: Autolyse refers to the initial rest period after combining the flour and water in your dough. During this time, the flour hydrates, and gluten development begins. It helps improve the dough's extensibility, resulting in a more open crumb structure.

b. Mixing and Bulk Fermentation: After the autolyse, you incorporate your sourdough starter into the dough and mix until well combined. The dough then goes through a period of bulk fermentation, where it rests and undergoes primary fermentation. Bulk fermentation allows the yeast and bacteria to convert the sugars in the dough into carbon dioxide and lactic acid, creating flavor, texture, and structure.

c. Folding: During bulk fermentation, you can incorporate folding techniques to strengthen the gluten structure and improve dough elasticity. Folding also helps distribute the yeast and bacteria evenly throughout the dough and expels any excess carbon dioxide.

d. Shaping and Final Proofing: After bulk fermentation, the dough is shaped into its desired form. This step involves gently shaping the dough to create tension and structure. The shaped dough then goes through the final proofing stage, where it rests and undergoes secondary fermentation. This final fermentation allows the dough to rise and develop more flavor.

Baking Your Sourdough Bread

Once the final proofing is complete, it's time to bake your sourdough bread! Baking sourdough requires a hot oven, steam, and proper timing to achieve the desired crust, crumb structure, and flavor. Here are the essential steps to baking your sourdough bread:

a. Preheating: Preheat your oven to a high temperature, typically around 450°F (230°C). Place a baking stone or a baking sheet on the middle rack to preheat as well. A hot oven and a preheated baking surface help create a crisp crust and promote oven spring.

b. Scoring: Before placing the dough in the oven, score the top surface with a sharp blade or a bread lame. Scoring allows the dough to expand during baking, creating a controlled release of steam and a visually appealing pattern on the crust.

c. Steam: Steam is crucial for creating a beautiful crust and promoting oven spring. You can generate steam by various methods, such as placing a tray of ice cubes in the bottom of the oven or spraying water onto the oven walls. The steam helps keep the dough's surface moist during the initial stages of baking.

d. Baking Time and Temperature: After introducing the dough to the hot oven, lower the temperature to around 400°F (200°C) to allow the bread to bake evenly without excessive browning. The exact baking time can vary depending on the size and shape of the loaf. A general guideline is to bake for around 30 to 40 minutes, but it's crucial to rely on visual cues such as a deep golden-brown crust and a hollow sound when tapped on the bottom to determine doneness.

e. Cooling and Enjoying: Once the bread is baked, remove it from the oven and transfer it to a wire rack to cool completely. Allow the bread to rest for at least an hour before slicing. This resting period allows the crumb to set and ensures a better texture.

Troubleshooting and Refining Techniques

Baking sourdough bread can be a rewarding yet challenging endeavor. As you gain more experience, you may encounter various issues and opportunities for refinement. Here are some common troubleshooting tips and refining techniques:

a. Overproofing: Overproofing occurs when the dough has fermented for too long, resulting in a collapsed or overly sour loaf. To avoid overproofing, closely monitor the dough during bulk fermentation and the final proofing stage. Look for signs of fermentation, such as increased volume, visible bubbles, and a slightly domed appearance.

b. Underproofing: Underproofing happens when the dough has not fermented enough, leading to a dense crumb and lack of flavor. To ensure proper proofing, consider factors such as ambient temperature, dough consistency, and the activity of your sourdough starter. Adjust the proofing time accordingly to achieve optimal results.

c. Oven Spring: Oven spring refers to the significant rise that occurs in the dough during the initial stages of baking. If your bread lacks oven spring, it could be due to several factors, including underproofing, inadequate gluten development, or insufficient steam in the oven. Experiment with adjusting proofing times, kneading techniques, and steam-generating methods to enhance oven spring.

d. Flavor Development: The flavor of your sourdough bread can be influenced by various factors, including the hydration level of the dough, the fermentation temperature, and the maturation of your sourdough starter. Experiment with different variables to achieve the desired balance of tanginess and depth of flavor.

e. Consistency and Hydration: The consistency and hydration level of your dough can significantly impact the texture and crumb structure of the bread. Experiment with different hydration levels to find your preferred balance between an open crumb and a manageable dough. Adjust the amount of water or flour during mixing and folding stages to achieve the desired consistency.

Remember, each loaf you bake presents an opportunity to refine your techniques and learn from the process. Be patient, persistent, and open to experimentation as you continue to hone your skills as a sourdough bread baker.

Advanced Sourdough Techniques

Once you have mastered the basics of sourdough bread baking, you can begin to explore advanced techniques to take your skills to the next level. Here are a few techniques you can experiment with:

a. Retarding the Dough: Retarding the dough refers to the process of refrigerating the shaped dough for an extended period, typically overnight, before baking. This technique allows the flavors to develop further and creates a more complex taste profile. Additionally, retarding the dough can also enhance the texture and improve the crust color during baking.

b. Pre-ferments: Pre-ferments, also known as levains or preferments, involve fermenting a portion of the flour, water, and sourdough starter for a specific time before incorporating it into the final dough. This technique enhances the flavor and texture of the bread, as the extended fermentation period allows the flavors to develop and the gluten to strengthen.

c. Multiple Feedings: Instead of feeding your sourdough starter once before baking, you can experiment with multiple feedings to enhance the flavor complexity. By feeding your starter two or more times before incorporating it into the dough, you allow it to develop a more pronounced and nuanced flavor profile.

d. Hybrid Loaves: Hybrid loaves combine the use of sourdough starter with a small amount of commercial yeast. This technique allows for more predictable and controlled fermentation while still enjoying the benefits of sourdough flavor and texture.

Shaping and Scoring Techniques

The shaping and scoring of your sourdough loaves not only contribute to their appearance but also play a vital role in the final texture and crumb structure. Here are some shaping and scoring techniques to experiment with:

a. Boule: The boule shape is a classic round loaf with a tight and even structure. To shape a boule, gently flatten the dough, then fold and tuck the edges towards the center, creating tension on the surface. Flip the dough and let it rest seam-side down before baking.

b. Batard: The batard shape is an elongated oval loaf with tapered ends. To shape a batard, flatten the dough into a rectangle, then fold the sides inward and roll it tightly from one end to the other. Pinch the seam to seal it and place the dough seam-side down for the final proofing.

c. Baguette: Baguettes are long and slender loaves with a thin, crispy crust. To shape a baguette, flatten the dough into a rectangle, then fold and roll it tightly from one end to the other. Stretch the dough gently to elongate it and place it on a floured couche or baguette pan for the final proofing.

d. Scoring: Scoring the surface of your dough before baking allows it to expand and release steam during the baking process. Use a sharp blade or bread lame to make shallow cuts or intricate patterns on the surface. Experiment with different scoring techniques to create visually appealing designs and control the rise of the loaf.

Specialty Sourdough Breads

Sourdough bread offers endless opportunities for creativity and experimentation. Here are a few specialty sourdough breads that you can explore:

a. Whole Grain Sourdough: Incorporate different whole grain flours like spelt, rye, or einkorn into your sourdough bread. These flours add unique flavors, textures, and nutritional value to your loaves.

b. Olive Sourdough: Add chopped or pitted olives to your dough for a savory and tangy twist. The briny flavors of olives pair exceptionally well with the sourness of the bread.

c. Cheese and Herb Sourdough: Introduce grated cheese, such as cheddar, Parmesan, or Gruyère, along with herbs like rosemary or thyme, to your dough. These additions create a bread with rich, savory flavors.

d. Cinnamon Raisin Sourdough: Sweeten your sourdough bread by incorporating cinnamon and raisins into the dough. The combination of the tangy sourdough and the sweet, aromatic filling is a delightful treat.

Troubleshooting and Refining Techniques
Even with experience, sourdough baking can present challenges. Here are some troubleshooting tips and refining techniques to help you overcome common issues:

a. Sourness Level: If your sourdough bread is not sour enough, try adjusting the fermentation time or temperature. A longer fermentation or a slightly higher temperature can intensify the sour flavors. Additionally, experimenting with different types of flour and hydration levels can also impact the sourness of the bread.

b. Oven Spring: If your bread lacks sufficient oven spring and doesn't achieve the desired rise, check the proofing time and temperature. Underproofing or overproofing can affect the dough's ability to rise in the oven. Adjust the proofing time accordingly to achieve optimal oven spring.

c. Crumb Structure: The crumb structure of your bread can be influenced by various factors, including hydration level, gluten development, and fermentation time. Experiment with different hydration levels, folding techniques, and fermentation schedules to achieve the desired open crumb or a denser, more even crumb.

d. Crust Color: If your crust is pale instead of deeply golden, try increasing the oven temperature during the initial stages of baking. A higher heat can promote browning and enhance the visual appeal of your bread.

e. Consistency and Hydration: Pay attention to the consistency and hydration level of your dough. Adjust the amount of water or flour during the mixing and folding stages to achieve the desired texture and dough handling properties. The right consistency contributes to a well-developed gluten structure and a more balanced crumb.

Flavor Variations: Exploring the Possibilities

One of the joys of sourdough baking is the ability to create a wide range of flavor variations. By incorporating different ingredients and techniques, you can customize your sourdough bread to suit your taste preferences. Here are a few flavor variations to explore:

a. Seeded Sourdough: Add a variety of seeds, such as sesame, sunflower, flax, or pumpkin seeds, to your dough. These seeds not only add a delightful crunch but also provide additional nutrition and flavor complexity to your bread.

b. Herb-Infused Sourdough: Incorporate fresh or dried herbs into your dough, such as rosemary, thyme, basil, or dill. The aromatic flavors of herbs infuse the bread, creating a delightful sensory experience.

c. Fruity Sourdough: Introduce dried or fresh fruits to your dough, such as raisins, cranberries, chopped apples, or apricots. The natural sweetness of the fruits complements the tangy flavor of sourdough, resulting in a delicious balance of flavors.

d. Nutty Sourdough: Experiment with different types of nuts, such as walnuts, almonds, or pecans, to add a nutty richness to your bread. Toast the nuts beforehand to enhance their flavors and textures.

e. Spiced Sourdough: Incorporate warm spices like cinnamon, nutmeg, or cardamom into your dough. These spices lend a cozy and aromatic touch to your bread, perfect for the colder months.

Gluten-free Sourdough

For individuals following a gluten-free diet, sourdough bread can still be enjoyed by using alternative flours. Gluten-free sourdough involves using flours like rice flour, buckwheat flour, sorghum flour, or a blend of gluten-free flours. While gluten-free sourdough may not have the same elasticity and structure as traditional sourdough, it can still offer a tangy flavor and a satisfying texture.

When working with gluten-free sourdough, it's important to consider the unique characteristics of gluten-free flours and their hydration requirements. Experimentation and adjusting the ratios of different flours may be necessary to achieve the desired texture and flavor.

Sourdough in Everyday Cooking

Sourdough isn't limited to bread alone. Its tangy flavor and unique fermentation qualities can enhance various dishes in your everyday cooking. Here are some ideas for incorporating sourdough into your meals:

a. Sourdough Pancakes or Waffles: Use sourdough starter as a leavening agent in your pancake or waffle batter. The sourdough adds a subtle tanginess and extra fluffiness to the final product.

b. Sourdough Pizza Dough: Substitute a portion of the flour in your pizza dough recipe with sourdough starter. The long fermentation process adds depth of flavor to the crust, resulting in a deliciously tangy and crispy pizza.

c. Sourdough Crackers: Use excess sourdough starter to make homemade sourdough crackers. Mix the starter with herbs, spices, or cheese, roll it out thinly, and bake until crispy. These crackers make for a delightful snack or accompaniment to cheese and dips.

d. Sourdough Discard Recipes: Don't let your excess sourdough starter go to waste! Look for recipes that utilize sourdough discard, such as pancakes, muffins, or even sourdough chocolate cake. These recipes allow you to enjoy the tangy flavors of sourdough in a variety of baked goods.

The Sourdough Community: Learning and Sharing

The world of sourdough bread-baking is vast and full of passionate bakers who are eager to share their knowledge and experiences. Engaging with the sourdough community can be a valuable source of inspiration, learning, and support. Here are a few ways to connect with the sourdough community:

a. Online Forums and Groups: Join online forums, social media groups, or dedicated sourdough baking communities to connect with like-minded bakers. Share your experiences, ask questions, and learn from the collective wisdom of the community.

b. Workshops and Classes: Attend sourdough workshops or classes to deepen your knowledge and refine your skills. These hands-on experiences offer an opportunity to learn from experienced instructors and connect with other baking enthusiasts.

c. Local Bakeries and Farmers' Markets: Visit local bakeries or farmers' markets that specialize in sourdough bread. Engage in conversations with the bakers, inquire about their techniques, and seek recommendations for further learning resources.

d. Sourdough Exchanges: Participate in sourdough exchanges where bakers share their starter cultures with each other. It's a wonderful way to experience different flavors and explore the diversity of sourdough bread.

Bread and Sourdough Mastery

By immersing yourself in the sourdough community, you can continue to learn, grow, and expand your horizons as a sourdough bread baker.

Sourdough for Health and Digestibility

Beyond its incredible flavors, sourdough bread offers potential health benefits and improved digestibility compared to commercially produced bread. The long fermentation process of sourdough breaks down complex carbohydrates, reduces phytic acid, and increases nutrient availability. Here are some of the key health benefits of eating sourdough:

a. Improved Digestibility: The natural fermentation process in sourdough breaks down proteins and starches, making them easier to digest. This can be particularly beneficial for individuals with gluten sensitivity or intolerance, as the fermentation process partially breaks down gluten proteins.

b. Increased Nutrient Absorption: Fermentation increases the bioavailability of vitamins and minerals present in the bread. The breakdown of phytic acid reduces its ability to bind to minerals, allowing for better absorption of nutrients by the body.

c. Lower Glycemic Index: Sourdough bread has a lower glycemic index compared to commercial bread. The slow fermentation process and the presence of organic acids contribute to a slower release of glucose into the bloodstream, helping to stabilize blood sugar levels.

d. Gut Health: The beneficial bacteria present in sourdough bread, such as lactobacilli, can promote a healthy gut microbiome. These bacteria may help improve digestion, boost immune function, and contribute to overall well-being.

Sourdough as a Sustainable Choice

Choosing sourdough bread can also be a more sustainable option compared to commercial bread. Here's why:

a. Reduced Waste: With a sourdough starter, you can maintain a perpetual fermentation process, eliminating the need for store-bought yeast for every loaf. This reduces packaging waste and reliance on single-use yeast packets.

b. Locally Sourced Ingredients: Sourdough baking often encourages the use of locally sourced, high-quality ingredients, such as locally grown grains or artisanal flours. Supporting local farmers and millers fosters a more sustainable and resilient food ecosystem.

c. Energy Efficiency: Sourdough bread typically requires longer fermentation times, allowing for slower rising and more flavor development. This slower process can be more energy-efficient compared to commercial bread production methods.

d. Reduced Chemical Inputs: Commercial bread often contains additives, preservatives, and dough conditioners. By baking your own sourdough bread, you have control over the ingredients used, ensuring a cleaner, more natural product without unnecessary chemicals.

Sourdough Troubleshooting: Common Issues and Solutions

As with any baking endeavor, sourdough bread baking can sometimes present challenges. Here are some common issues and their possible solutions:

a. Dense Loaf: A dense loaf can be the result of insufficient gluten development or underproofing. Ensure adequate kneading or stretching and folding during bulk fermentation to develop a strong gluten structure. Allow the dough to properly proof until it has increased in volume and shows good fermentation activity.

b. Lack of Oven Spring: Oven spring refers to the significant rise that occurs during the initial stages of baking. If your loaf lacks oven spring, it may be due to underproofing, insufficient gluten development, or low oven temperature. Adjust your proofing times, improve gluten development through adequate kneading, and ensure proper oven preheating.

c. Sourdough Bread with Large Holes: Large holes or irregular crumb structure can result from excessive fermentation or overproofing. To achieve a more even crumb, reduce the proofing time or adjust the fermentation temperature to slow down the fermentation process.

d. Sourdough Bread with Gummy Crumb: A gummy crumb can indicate underbaking. Ensure that your bread is baked for an adequate amount of time, allowing it to reach the proper internal temperature.

Remember that troubleshooting is part of the learning process, and with practice, you will develop a deeper understanding of your dough and the necessary adjustments to achieve the desired results.

Conclusion

In this chapter, we have delved into the world of sourdough bread, exploring its health benefits, digestibility, sustainability, and troubleshooting tips. Sourdough bread not only offers exceptional flavors and textures but also provides a host of advantages that contribute to a healthier and more sustainable lifestyle.

Chapter 6

Sourdough Science: Exploring Fermentation and Flavor

In *The Definitive Bread and Sourdough Recipe Cookbook,* we embark on an exciting journey into the intricate world of sourdough science. We will delve deep into the process of fermentation and explore how it shapes the flavors, textures, and overall quality of sourdough bread. By understanding the scientific principles at work, you will gain valuable insights that will empower you to become a master of sourdough baking. So, let's dive into the fascinating realm of sourdough fermentation and flavor.

The Science of Fermentation: Unleashing the Power of Microorganisms

At the heart of sourdough baking lies the process of fermentation, driven by a dynamic community of microorganisms. Yeasts and lactic acid bacteria (LAB) are the primary players in this microbial orchestra. Let's explore their roles and the scientific processes they undergo during fermentation.

a. Yeasts: Yeasts are single-celled fungi that belong to the *Saccharomyces* genus, with *Saccharomyces cerevisiae* being the predominant species in sourdough. These microscopic organisms feed on sugars in the dough and undergo alcoholic fermentation, converting sugars into carbon dioxide and alcohol. The carbon dioxide produced creates the characteristic rise and airy structure of sourdough bread, while the alcohol evaporates during baking.

b. Lactic Acid Bacteria (LAB): LAB are a group of bacteria that include strains such as *Lactobacillus sanfranciscensis, Lactobacillus brevis,* and *Lactobacillus plantarum,* among others. They are responsible for the lactic acid fermentation process that contributes to the tangy flavor and extended shelf life of sourdough bread. LAB produce lactic acid as a byproduct of metabolizing carbohydrates, which contributes to the distinctive sour taste and also acts as a natural preservative.

The Fermentation Process: A Symphony of Biochemical Reactions

During fermentation, a multitude of biochemical reactions occur within the dough, transforming its composition and yielding unique flavors and textures. Let's explore some of the key processes that take place during sourdough fermentation:

a. Carbohydrate Metabolism: Yeasts and LAB break down complex carbohydrates, such as starches, into simpler sugars through enzymatic processes. The yeast enzymes, specifically amylases, hydrolyze starch molecules into fermentable sugars. LAB, on the other hand, ferment sugars into lactic acid.

b. Acidification: As LAB consume sugars, they produce lactic acid as a metabolic byproduct. This acidification process lowers the dough's pH, creating an acidic environment that inhibits the growth of undesirable microorganisms while promoting the development of desired flavors and textures.

c. Gluten Development: Gluten, the protein network responsible for the structure and elasticity of bread, undergoes changes during fermentation. The enzymes released by yeasts and LAB break down gluten proteins, making them more extensible and contributing to the development of a desirable crumb structure.

d. Flavor Compound Formation: Fermentation generates a wide array of flavor compounds that contribute to the complex taste profile of sourdough bread. During yeast fermentation, alcohol, esters, and other volatile compounds are produced, adding fruity, nutty, and aromatic notes. LAB, with their lactic acid production, contribute tanginess and enhance the overall flavor.

The Influence of Time and Temperature: Controlling Fermentation Dynamics

The duration and temperature of fermentation significantly impact the flavor, texture, and overall quality of sourdough bread. By understanding how time and temperature affect the fermentation process, you can fine-tune your baking techniques to achieve the desired results. Here are key factors to consider:

a. Fermentation Time: Longer fermentation allows for more extensive flavor development as the microorganisms have more time to metabolize sugars and produce aromatic compounds. It also contributes to a more relaxed gluten structure, resulting in a lighter and more open crumb. However, prolonged fermentation can also lead to over-fermentation, causing an excessively sour or collapsed loaf.

b. Temperature Control: The temperature at which fermentation occurs influences the activity and growth of yeasts and LAB. Cooler temperatures slow down fermentation, allowing for more control over the process and promoting the development of complex flavors. Warmer temperatures accelerate fermentation but may lead to a quicker depletion of sugars and a more pronounced sourness.

c. Autolyse: Autolyse is a technique that involves resting the dough for a period before the addition of salt and sourdough starter. This rest period allows the flour to fully hydrate and initiates enzymatic activity, promoting gluten development and flavor formation.

d. Retardation: Retarding the dough by refrigerating it for a specific duration can further enhance flavor and texture. Cold fermentation slows down enzymatic activity and extends the fermentation time, leading to a more pronounced tanginess and a more complex flavor profile.

Flavor Factors: Understanding the Variables at Play

A multitude of variables influence the flavor of sourdough bread. By understanding these factors, you can manipulate them to achieve specific flavor profiles. Let's explore some key variables that shape the taste of your sourdough creations:

a. Flour Selection: Different types of flour, such as wheat, rye, spelt, or even alternative flours like einkorn or buckwheat, impart unique flavors and characteristics to sourdough bread. Experimenting with different flours can result in a diverse range of flavors and textures.

b. Hydration Level: The hydration level of the dough affects gluten development, crumb structure, and flavor. A higher hydration level can contribute to a more open crumb and a lighter texture, while a lower hydration level can result in a denser crumb and a chewier texture.

c. Sourdough Starter Maturation: The maturity of your sourdough starter significantly influences the flavors it imparts to the bread. A well-matured starter, with regular feedings and a consistent fermentation routine, develops a more complex flavor profile.

d. Feeding Schedule: Altering the feeding schedule of your sourdough starter can affect its acidity and flavor. Adjusting the frequency and ratio of feedings can create variations in sourness, tanginess, and overall flavor intensity.

e. Fermentation Container: The vessel in which the dough ferments can impact the flavors. Clay or ceramic containers may provide a more humid environment, resulting in a softer crust and a distinct flavor profile.

The Impact of Enzymes: Unlocking Flavor Potential

Enzymes play a crucial role in the biochemical reactions that occur during fermentation, and they can influence the flavor development of sourdough bread. Let's explore some key enzymes and their effects:

a. Amylase: Amylase enzymes break down starch into simpler sugars that yeasts and LAB can ferment. These enzymes contribute to the availability of fermentable sugars, affecting the rate and intensity of fermentation.

b. Protease: Protease enzymes break down proteins, including gluten, during fermentation. This enzymatic activity contributes to the development of a more extensible gluten structure, resulting in a lighter and more open crumb.

c. Lipase: Lipase enzymes can contribute to the development of desirable flavors by breaking down fats and releasing fatty acids. These fatty acids add depth and complexity to the taste profile of sourdough bread.

d. Phytase: Phytase enzymes are involved in breaking down phytic acid, a naturally occurring compound found in grains that can inhibit the absorption of certain minerals. By breaking down phytic acid, phytase enzymes increase the bioavailability of minerals, making them more accessible for absorption by the body.

Managing Fermentation: Techniques for Flavor Control

As a sourdough baker, you have the power to manipulate fermentation to achieve specific flavor profiles. Here are some techniques you can employ to control and enhance the flavors of your sourdough bread:

a. Levain Development: Pay attention to the fermentation stage of your levain, the pre-fermented portion of dough containing the sourdough starter. Allowing the levain to fully ripen before incorporating it into the final dough promotes optimal flavor development.

b. Bulk Fermentation: Adjust the duration and temperature of the bulk fermentation stage to fine-tune the flavors. Longer fermentation times and cooler temperatures generally result in more pronounced and complex flavors, while shorter times and warmer temperatures yield milder flavors.

c. Folding Technique: Implementing regular folds during the bulk fermentation stage helps to strengthen the gluten structure and distribute the fermentation byproducts, contributing to an even flavor throughout the dough.

d. Scoring: The way you score the dough before baking can also influence flavor development. Deep scores allow for greater expansion and the release of aromatic compounds during baking, enhancing the overall flavor.

e. Retarding the Dough: By retarding the dough in the refrigerator for an extended period, you can promote the development of deeper flavors. This slow fermentation process allows the microorganisms to continue their work, resulting in a more complex and nuanced taste.

The Maillard Reaction: Enhancing Flavor and Aroma

In addition to fermentation, the Maillard reaction plays a crucial role in creating the rich flavors and aromas of sourdough bread. This non-enzymatic browning reaction occurs between amino acids and reducing sugars when exposed to heat. Here's how the Maillard reaction contributes to the flavor of your bread:

a. Crust Formation: During baking, the heat triggers the Maillard reaction on the surface of the dough, leading to the formation of a crust with a deep golden-brown color. This crust adds texture and enhances the overall sensory experience of the bread.

b. Flavor Development: The Maillard reaction produces a range of flavor compounds, including aromatic molecules that contribute to the characteristic nutty, toasty, and caramel-like flavors of crusty bread.

c. Aroma Release: The Maillard reaction also releases volatile compounds that contribute to the enticing aroma of freshly baked sourdough bread. These compounds stimulate our olfactory senses and enhance the overall enjoyment of the bread.

Flavor Enhancement Techniques
In addition to understanding the science behind fermentation and the Maillard reaction, there are several techniques you can employ to enhance the flavor of your sourdough bread:

a. Preferments: Pre-ferments, such as a poolish or a biga, are often used to develop more complex flavors. These pre-fermented doughs are made by mixing a portion of the flour, water, and a small amount of sourdough starter and allowing them to ferment for a specific time. The longer fermentation period increases flavor development and can contribute to a richer taste.

b. Flavor Additions: Experiment with adding flavor-boosting ingredients to your dough, such as herbs, spices, nuts, seeds, or dried fruits. These additions can infuse your bread with new and exciting flavors that complement the tanginess of the sourdough.

c. Retained Dough: Retaining a portion of the dough from a previous batch and incorporating it into the next batch, known as "old dough" or "chef," can intensify the flavor. This technique introduces matured microorganisms from the previous dough, contributing to a more robust and pronounced taste.

d. Long Cold Fermentation: By extending the fermentation time and retarding the dough in the refrigerator, you can develop complex flavors and enhance the tanginess of your bread. This technique allows the microorganisms to work slowly, promoting deeper flavor development.

The Impact of Flour: Unleashing the Potential

The choice of flour plays a significant role in the flavor profile of sourdough bread. Different types of flour, from different grains or milled from different parts of the grain, impart distinct flavors and textures to the final product. Here are some common types of flour used in sourdough baking and their flavor characteristics:

a. Wheat Flour: Wheat flour is the most common choice for sourdough bread baking. It offers a delicate, nutty flavor with a hint of sweetness. Whole wheat flour adds depth and a rustic quality to the bread, while bread flour lends a lighter texture and a milder flavor.

b. Rye Flour: Rye flour introduces a unique and robust flavor to sourdough bread. It has a distinct tanginess and a rich, earthy taste. Rye flour also contributes to a denser crumb and a darker color.

c. Spelt Flour: Spelt flour, an ancient grain, imparts a mild, nutty flavor to sourdough bread. It is often favored for its digestibility and gentle taste.

d. Alternative Flours: Experimenting with alternative flours, such as einkorn, emmer, or kamut, can introduce novel flavors and textures to your bread. These ancient grains offer their own distinct characteristics and can contribute to a more diverse sourdough experience.

The Art of Flavor Balance

Achieving a harmonious flavor balance is a crucial aspect of sourdough baking. It involves striking a careful equilibrium between the tanginess of sourdough and other flavors in the bread. Here are some considerations for achieving a well-balanced flavor profile:

a. Sourness Level: The sourness of sourdough bread can be adjusted by manipulating the fermentation time and temperature. Longer fermentation and cooler temperatures generally result in more pronounced tanginess, while shorter fermentation and warmer temperatures yield milder flavors.

b. Sweetness and Nuttiness: Adding a touch of sweetness or incorporating ingredients with a nutty flavor can balance the tanginess of sourdough. Honey, molasses, or toasted nuts can complement the sour flavors and add depth and complexity to the overall taste.

c. Salt: Salt is not only a flavor enhancer but also an essential ingredient in bread baking. It helps to balance the acidity of sourdough and enhance the overall flavor profile. Experiment with different types of salt to find the one that best complements the flavors of your bread.

d. Aromatics: Consider the addition of aromatic ingredients such as herbs, spices, or citrus zest to add layers of complexity and balance to the flavor profile of your sourdough bread. These aromatic components can create a sensory delight and contribute to a more well-rounded taste.

The Influence of Water: The Forgotten Ingredient

While flour, yeast, and bacteria often steal the spotlight in sourdough baking, the importance of water cannot be overlooked. Water serves as the medium for activating enzymes, dissolving sugars, and facilitating microbial activity. Here are some considerations regarding water and its impact on fermentation and flavor:

a. Water Quality: The quality of water used in sourdough baking can affect the final flavor of the bread. Chlorinated tap water, for example, can hinder microbial activity and impart undesirable flavors. Using filtered or spring water can help maintain a more neutral taste and support optimal fermentation.

b. Hydration Ratio: The hydration ratio, or the amount of water in relation to flour, plays a vital role in dough development and fermentation. Adjusting the hydration level can influence the texture, crumb structure, and overall flavor of the bread. Higher hydration levels tend to yield a more open crumb and contribute to a lighter, airier texture.

c. Mineral Content: The mineral content of water can vary depending on its source. Minerals present in water, such as calcium and magnesium, can affect enzyme activity and gluten development. Experimenting with different types of water and observing the impact on fermentation and flavor can provide valuable insights.

The Role of Time: Aging and Flavor Development

Just as fine wine and cheese benefit from aging, so does sourdough bread. The process of aging sourdough dough allows for the development of deeper flavors and enhanced aromas. Here are a few techniques that utilize time to optimize flavor:

a. Cold Fermentation: Retarding the dough in the refrigerator for an extended period, typically overnight or longer, can lead to more pronounced flavors. This slow fermentation process allows for the gradual release of flavors and the development of complex taste profiles.

b. Aging the Levain: Allowing the sourdough starter to mature and age before incorporating it into the dough can intensify the flavors. A well-matured starter, with regular feedings and consistent fermentation, builds a robust and well-rounded flavor profile.

c. Pre-ferments: Pre-fermented doughs, such as poolish or biga, are essentially aged doughs that contribute to flavor development. These pre-ferments are made by combining a portion of the flour, water, and starter and allowing them to ferment for a specific duration. The extended fermentation time allows for the accumulation of flavors, resulting in a more complex taste.

Beyond Fermentation: Other Factors Influencing Flavor

While fermentation is the cornerstone of sourdough flavor development, other factors can also impact the taste profile of your bread. Here are a few additional considerations:

a. Oven Spring: The initial rise of the dough in the oven, known as oven spring, is critical for achieving the desired texture and crumb structure. Proper oven spring allows for optimal expansion and the release of aromatic compounds, enhancing the overall flavor.

b. Baking Temperature and Time: The temperature at which you bake your sourdough bread affects the development of flavor. A higher baking temperature can promote browning and caramelization, contributing to a richer flavor profile. The baking time also influences flavor, as a longer bake can deepen the flavors and create a more pronounced crust.

c. Resting Period: Allowing the bread to rest for a period after baking, typically referred to as "oven-spring rest" or "oven-spring recovery," can further develop the flavors. This rest period allows for moisture redistribution and the stabilization of the crumb structure, resulting in a more enjoyable eating experience.

d. Storage Conditions: How you store your sourdough bread after baking can influence its flavor over time. Properly storing bread in a breathable bag or paper can help maintain its crust integrity while allowing it to develop further flavors through natural aging.

The Power of Your Senses: Flavor Perception

Lastly, as you continue your sourdough baking journey, remember to engage all your senses in the process. Flavor perception is a multisensory experience that involves not only taste but also aroma, texture, and visual presentation. Here are a few tips to fully embrace the sensory aspects of your sourdough creations:

a. Smell: Take a moment to inhale the aroma of freshly baked sourdough bread. The complex combination of yeasty notes, nutty undertones, and caramelized scents creates a sensory delight.

b. Taste: Pay attention to the interplay of flavors on your palate. Notice the tanginess, sweetness, and subtle nuances that make each mouthful unique.

c. Texture: Appreciate the contrast between the crisp crust and the tender, airy crumb. Note the chewiness, lightness, and overall mouthfeel.

d. Visual Appeal: Feast your eyes on the beautifully scored crust, the golden-brown color, and the intricate patterns created during baking. The visual presentation adds to the overall enjoyment of your sourdough bread.

Bread and Sourdough Mastery

Unlocking Complexity: Flavor Variations in Sourdough

One of the fascinating aspects of sourdough baking is the wide range of flavor variations that can be achieved. Factors such as fermentation time, temperature, hydration level, and ingredient selection can all contribute to unique flavor profiles. Let's explore some common flavor variations and how they can be achieved:

a. Mild and Balanced: If you prefer a milder flavor, you can shorten the fermentation time and use a higher ratio of wheat flour to create a well-balanced and subtly tangy bread.

b. Tangy and Robust: For those seeking a more pronounced tanginess, extending the fermentation time and using a higher ratio of sourdough starter can intensify the sour flavor. Cooler temperatures during fermentation can also contribute to a stronger tang.

c. Nutty and Sweet: Adding ingredients such as toasted nuts, seeds, or even a touch of honey or maple syrup can enhance the nutty and sweet flavors in your bread. Experimenting with different flours, such as spelt or rye, can also add depth and complexity.

d. Herbal and Savory: Incorporating herbs, spices, or even cheese into your dough can infuse it with delightful savory flavors. Consider ingredients like rosemary, thyme, garlic, or Parmesan to create bread with a savory twist.

e. Fruity and Aromatic: Dried fruits, such as raisins or cranberries, can bring a touch of sweetness and fruitiness to your bread. Adding citrus zest or a hint of cinnamon can also contribute to a delightful aroma and flavor.

Understanding Your Preferences: Experiment and Taste

Ultimately, developing a deep understanding of flavor in sourdough bread comes down to experimentation and tasting. Each baker's preferences are unique, and by exploring different variables and techniques, you can fine-tune your sourdough to suit your personal taste. Here are a few tips to help you along the way:

a. Keep Detailed Notes: Document your recipes, fermentation times, and observations about flavor development. This will allow you to track your progress and make informed adjustments.

b. Conduct Comparative Tastings: Bake multiple loaves using different variables and taste them side by side. This comparative approach will help you discern the subtle differences and better understand the impact of each variable.

c. Seek Feedback: Share your bread with friends, family, or fellow bakers and ask for their feedback. Different perspectives can provide valuable insights and open up new avenues for flavor exploration.

d. Embrace Iteration: Remember that achieving the perfect flavor takes time and practice. Don't be afraid to experiment, make adjustments, and iterate on your recipes to continuously improve and refine your sourdough bread.

Exploring Regional and Cultural Variations

Sourdough bread is not only a culinary delight but also a reflection of regional and cultural traditions. Different regions around the world have their unique approaches to sourdough baking, resulting in a diverse array of flavors and techniques. Let's explore some of these regional variations and the flavors they bring:

a. San Francisco Sourdough: San Francisco is renowned for its sourdough bread, characterized by a tangy flavor and a distinctive aroma. The unique combination of local yeast strains and bacteria, along with the cool climate, contributes to the signature flavor profile.

b. French Sourdough (Pain au Levain): The French have mastered the art of producing delectable sourdough bread. Pain au Levain, with its mildly tangy flavor, chewy crumb, and crispy crust, is a testament to their expertise.

c. German Rye Sourdough: Germany is famous for its hearty and flavorful rye bread. The combination of rye flour, sourdough starter, and a long fermentation process gives German rye bread its characteristic tanginess and dense crumb.

d. Italian Sourdough (Pane Casereccio): Italian sourdough bread, known as Pane Casereccio, features a crusty exterior, a soft and chewy crumb, and a balanced sourness. It is often made with a mixture of wheat and rye flours, resulting in a complex and delightful flavor.

e. Nordic Sourdough (Ruisleipä): Nordic countries, such as Finland and Sweden, have their own sourdough bread traditions. Ruisleipä, a Finnish rye bread, has a dark color, a rich flavor, and a slightly sweet and tangy taste. It is often enjoyed with traditional Nordic toppings like butter, cheese, or fish.

The Impact of Grains and Alternative Flours

While wheat is the most commonly used grain in sourdough baking, there is a growing interest in incorporating alternative flours and grains. These alternative options offer unique flavors, textures, and nutritional profiles. Let's explore some popular alternative flours and their impact on sourdough flavor:

a. Spelt Flour: Spelt is an ancient grain that has gained popularity due to its nutty flavor and easier digestibility. When used in sourdough bread, spelt flour adds a delicate sweetness and a distinct aroma.

b. Kamut Flour: Kamut, also known as Khorasan wheat, is an ancient grain with a buttery and slightly nutty flavor. Kamut flour can bring a rich and distinctive taste to your sourdough bread.

c. Einkorn Flour: Einkorn is one of the oldest cultivated grains and has a unique, earthy flavor. Baking with einkorn flour can result in bread with a delicate and subtly sweet taste.

d. Gluten-Free Flours: Individuals with gluten sensitivities can still enjoy sourdough bread by using gluten-free flours such as rice flour, buckwheat flour, or teff flour. These flours bring their own flavors and textures, allowing for a diverse range of gluten-free sourdough creations.

The Impact of Seasonality and Locally Sourced Ingredients

Seasonality and locally sourced ingredients can have a significant impact on the flavors of your sourdough bread. Using fresh, local ingredients that are in season can enhance the taste and contribute to a sense of connection with your surroundings. Here are some ways to incorporate seasonality into your sourdough baking:

a. Seasonal Fruits and Vegetables: Incorporate seasonal fruits or vegetables into your sourdough bread, either by adding them directly to the dough or creating fillings and swirls. For example, you can use fresh berries in the summer or roasted pumpkin in the fall to infuse unique flavors into your bread.

b. Herbs and Spices: Experiment with fresh herbs and spices that are readily available during different seasons. Whether it's using fragrant rosemary in the winter or zesty lemon zest in the spring, these additions can elevate the flavor of your sourdough bread.

c. Local Flours and Grains: Consider using locally sourced flours and grains, which often have distinct flavors and characteristics. Supporting local farmers and millers not only contributes to the community but also allows you to explore the unique flavors of your region.

d. Wild Foraging: For the adventurous bakers, incorporating wild-foraged ingredients into your sourdough bread can be quite a thrilling experience. From wild mushrooms to edible flowers, there is a wide variety of flavors to discover in nature.

Balancing Tradition and Innovation

Sourdough baking is an art that embraces both tradition and innovation. While honoring the time-tested techniques that have been passed down through generations, there is also room for experimentation and pushing the boundaries of flavor. Here are some ways to balance tradition and innovation in your sourdough baking:

a. Respect the Fundamentals: Develop a solid foundation in sourdough baking by mastering the traditional techniques and understanding the principles behind fermentation and flavor development. This knowledge will serve as a guide as you explore new flavors and techniques.

b. Embrace New Ingredients and Techniques: Don't be afraid to incorporate new ingredients or explore innovative techniques. Whether it's using unique flours, introducing new fermentation methods, or incorporating unconventional flavor combinations, experimentation can lead to exciting discoveries.

c. Stay Connected with the Sourdough Community: Engaging with fellow bakers and participating in sourdough baking communities can provide inspiration, guidance, and opportunities to learn from others. Sharing experiences and ideas can foster a spirit of innovation and creativity in your own baking.

The Influence of Baking Equipment

The equipment you use in sourdough baking can also impact the fermentation and flavor of your bread. Here are some key elements to consider:

a. Dutch Oven: Baking your sourdough bread in a Dutch oven creates a controlled environment with trapped steam, resulting in a beautiful crust and enhanced flavor. The steam helps to create a moist baking environment, allowing the bread to expand fully and develop a desirable texture.

b. Baking Stone or Steel: Using a baking stone or steel can help distribute heat evenly, resulting in better oven spring and a more uniform crust. These tools also help to create a crispier crust, enhancing the overall flavor and texture of the bread.

c. Bread Cloche: A bread cloche, or bread dome, is a ceramic or clay baking vessel that replicates the steam-creating effects of a Dutch oven. It can produce similar results, with a crusty exterior and a moist crumb, contributing to a flavorful and well-textured loaf.

d. Banneton Proofing Baskets: Proofing your sourdough bread in banneton baskets, often made of natural materials like cane or rattan, can impart texture and design onto the crust. These baskets allow the dough to maintain its shape during the final rise, resulting in a visually appealing loaf.

e. Lame or Razor Blade: Using a lame or razor blade to score the dough before baking not only creates decorative patterns but also serves a functional purpose. Proper scoring allows the dough to expand and release steam, contributing to an optimal rise and enhanced flavor development.

Flavor Development Beyond Bread: Sourdough Discard

Sourdough discard refers to the portion of sourdough starter that is removed and discarded during the feeding process. Instead of wasting this discard, it can be repurposed to create a variety of flavorful and delicious treats. Here are some ideas for utilizing sourdough discard:

a. Sourdough Pancakes: Incorporating sourdough discard into pancake batter adds a tangy flavor and a fluffy texture. These pancakes can be enjoyed with a drizzle of maple syrup or topped with fresh fruits and yogurt.

b. Sourdough Waffles: Similar to pancakes, sourdough discard can be used to make light and crispy waffles. Serve them with your favorite toppings, such as berries, whipped cream, or a dusting of powdered sugar.

c. Sourdough Crackers: Mixing sourdough discard with flour, oil, and seasonings creates a flavorful dough that can be rolled out and baked into crispy, savory crackers. Experiment with different herbs and spices to customize the flavors.

d. Sourdough Pretzels: The tanginess of sourdough discard can elevate homemade pretzels, giving them a unique flavor profile. Sprinkle them with coarse salt or serve them with a dipping sauce for a satisfying snack.

e. Sourdough Biscuits or Scones: Incorporate sourdough discard into biscuit or scone dough to add a subtle tang and improve the texture. These treats are perfect for breakfast or as accompaniments to soups and stews.

Exploring Sweet Sourdough Treats
Sourdough isn't limited to savory creations. It can also be used to make delicious sweet treats that showcase the complex flavors of fermentation. Here are some sweet sourdough ideas to satisfy your sweet tooth:

a. Sourdough Cinnamon Rolls: Enriched with butter, sugar, and cinnamon, sourdough cinnamon rolls have a tangy twist that enhances the sweetness and adds depth to the flavors. The luscious cream cheese icing complements the tanginess perfectly.

b. Sourdough Chocolate Chip Cookies: Incorporating sourdough discard into your chocolate chip cookie dough can result in cookies with a delightful tang and a soft, chewy texture. The tanginess cuts through the sweetness, creating a well-balanced treat.

c. Sourdough Banana Bread: Adding sourdough discard to your favorite banana bread recipe can add complexity and depth to the flavors. The tanginess of the sourdough complements the sweetness of the bananas, resulting in a moist and flavorful loaf.

d. Sourdough Coffee Cake: Sourdough discard can be incorporated into a tender and moist coffee cake batter. The tanginess of the sourdough pairs well with the coffee streusel topping, creating a delightful balance of flavors.

e. Sourdough Doughnuts: Sourdough discard can be used to create a flavorful doughnut batter. Fry them until golden brown and coat them in powdered sugar, glaze, or your favorite toppings for a unique twist on a classic treat.

Conclusion

In Chapter 6, we have explored the fascinating world of sourdough science, diving into the processes of fermentation and flavor development. From understanding the variables that influence fermentation to exploring the impact of grains, equipment, and alternative uses for sourdough discard, you have gained a deeper appreciation for the complexity of flavor in sourdough baking.

By embracing the scientific principles behind sourdough and incorporating innovative techniques and ingredients, you can create bread with unique flavor profiles that satisfy your palate. Whether you're exploring regional variations, experimenting with alternative flours, or indulging in sweet sourdough treats, the possibilities for flavor exploration are endless.

Chapter 7

Kneading and Shaping: The Artistry of Bread

In this chapter, we will explore the artistry of bread-shaping and the essential technique of kneading. Kneading is a crucial step in bread-making that develops gluten, strengthens the dough, and contributes to the desired texture and structure of the final loaf. Shaping, on the other hand, allows bakers to unleash their creativity, turning a ball of dough into a visually stunning work of art. Join us as we delve into the techniques, tips, and creative possibilities of kneading and shaping bread.

The Importance of Kneading:

Kneading is the process of working the dough to develop gluten, which gives bread its structure and texture. Here's why kneading is essential:

a. Gluten Development: Gluten, a protein complex, provides elasticity and strength to the dough. Kneading aligns and strengthens gluten strands, creating a network that traps carbon dioxide gas produced during fermentation, resulting in a well-risen loaf with a desirable crumb.

b. Dough Cohesion: Kneading evenly distributes moisture throughout the dough, promoting proper hydration and improving dough cohesion. It helps ensure that all ingredients are fully integrated and that the dough comes together into a smooth, cohesive mass.

c. Enzyme Activation: Kneading activates enzymes present in the flour, initiating biochemical reactions that contribute to flavor development and dough maturation. These reactions improve the flavor, color, and overall quality of the bread.

Kneading Techniques:

There are various kneading techniques to choose from, depending on the recipe and your personal preference. Here are some commonly used techniques:

a. Hand Kneading: Hand kneading is a traditional and tactile approach that allows you to intimately connect with the dough. Follow these steps for hand kneading:

i. Start with a lightly floured surface and place the dough on it.

ii. Using the heels of your hands, push the dough away from you, folding it over itself.

iii. Give the dough a quarter turn and repeat the process.

iv. Continue kneading, periodically turning the dough and incorporating flour if needed, until it becomes smooth, elastic, and slightly tacky.

b. Stand Mixer Kneading: Utilizing a stand mixer with a dough hook attachment can streamline the kneading process. Follow these steps for stand mixer kneading:

i. Place the dough in the mixing bowl fitted with the dough hook attachment.

ii. Start the mixer on low speed to combine the ingredients, then gradually increase to medium speed.

iii. Allow the dough hook to knead the dough for the specified duration, usually 8–10 minutes, until the dough is smooth, elastic, and slightly tacky.

c. Stretch and Fold Technique: The stretch and fold technique is an alternative to traditional kneading. It involves gently stretching the dough, folding it over itself, and repeating the process at intervals during the fermentation process. This technique helps develop gluten while minimizing oxidation and preserving the dough's gas-retaining properties.

Signs of Properly Kneaded Dough:

It's important to recognize the signs that indicate your dough has been properly kneaded. Here are some indicators to look for:

a. Smooth Texture: Well-kneaded dough will have a smooth, uniform texture. It should no longer feel sticky or excessively tacky to the touch.

b. Elasticity: Properly kneaded dough will exhibit elasticity, allowing it to stretch without tearing. When gently pulled, it should be able to stretch thin without breaking.

c. Windowpane Test: To check gluten development, perform the windowpane test. Take a small piece of dough and gently stretch it between your fingers. If the dough can be stretched thin enough to let light pass through without tearing, it has reached the desired gluten development.

d. Dough Temperature: During kneading, friction generates heat. The dough's temperature should increase slightly, indicating that the yeast is active and fermentation is progressing. Monitor the dough's temperature to ensure it stays within the ideal range for fermentation.

Artistic Shaping Techniques:

Shaping dough is where creativity takes center stage. Bakers can experiment with various techniques to create unique and visually appealing bread. Here are some popular shaping techniques:

a. Boule: Boule, or round loaf, is one of the most classic and versatile shapes. It involves tucking and pulling the dough edges towards the center to form a tight, round shape. This technique is commonly used for rustic, country-style bread.

b. Batard: Batard, or torpedo loaf, is an elongated shape with tapered ends. To achieve this shape, flatten the dough into a rectangle, fold in the sides, and roll it tightly from top to bottom, creating a cylinder shape.

c. Baguette: Baguette is a thin, elongated loaf with a crisp crust and an open crumb. To shape a baguette, flatten the dough into a rectangle, fold it in thirds like a letter, and roll it tightly from top to bottom, elongating it as you go.

d. Fougasse: Fougasse is a decorative, leaf-shaped bread that originates from France. After dividing the dough, make a series of cuts and openings to create a leaf-like pattern. This technique allows for artistic expression and creates an attractive centerpiece.

e. Braided Bread: Braided bread adds a touch of elegance to the table. Divide the dough into strands, braid them together, and join the ends to create a beautiful, woven loaf. This technique is often used for special occasions or festive breads.

Shaping Tips and Tricks:
To achieve optimal shaping results, consider these helpful tips:

a. Surface Tension: When shaping, ensure the dough has sufficient surface tension. Tightly seal any seams or openings to prevent the dough from spreading or losing its shape during proofing and baking.

b. Flour or Water: Use a small amount of flour or water on your hands or work surface to prevent sticking. Be cautious not to use too much flour, as it can hinder proper shaping or alter the hydration balance in the dough.

c. Resting Periods: Allow the dough to rest periodically during shaping. This helps relax the gluten and makes it more pliable, allowing for easier manipulation and better shape retention.

d. Practice and Patience: Shaping bread takes practice and patience. Don't be discouraged if your first attempts don't turn out perfectly. With time and experience, your shaping skills will improve, and you'll develop your unique style.

Decorative and Advanced Shaping Techniques:

For those looking to take their bread-shaping skills to the next level, there are advanced techniques that allow for even more intricate and decorative designs. These techniques require practice and precision but can result in stunning bread creations. Here are a few examples:

a. Spiral Shape: The spiral shape involves rolling the dough into a log and then coiling it tightly to create a beautiful spiral pattern. This technique works well for enriched dough or breads with fillings.

b. Braided Challah: Challah is a traditional Jewish bread known for its braided appearance. The dough is divided into strands and intricately braided, resulting in an impressive loaf that is as visually appealing as it is delicious.

c. Artisanal Patterns: Using a sharp knife or a scoring tool, you can create intricate patterns on the surface of the bread. This allows for artistic expression and can include geometric designs, floral motifs, or even personalized patterns.

d. Stuffed or Filled Breads: Experiment with creating stuffed or filled breads where the dough is wrapped around a savory or sweet filling. From cheese-filled breadsticks to cinnamon roll-inspired swirls, the possibilities are endless.

Troubleshooting Shaping Issues:

Shaping bread can sometimes present challenges, but with a few troubleshooting techniques, you can overcome common issues. Here are some tips for troubleshooting shaping problems:

a. Sticky Dough: If the dough is overly sticky and difficult to handle, it may indicate excessive hydration. Dust your hands and work surface lightly with flour, but avoid using too much flour, as it can affect the dough's texture and final result.

b. Collapsing Loaves: If your loaves tend to collapse or spread during proofing or baking, it could be due to underdeveloped gluten or insufficient tension during shaping. Ensure that the dough is properly kneaded, and create a tight surface tension when shaping to provide structural support.

c. Uneven Shape: To achieve an even shape, pay attention to the tension and symmetry while shaping. Take your time and practice gentle handling to prevent tearing or deflating the dough. If needed, rest the dough and allow it to relax before continuing with shaping.

d. Loaves Bursting: Bursting or splitting of loaves during baking may indicate insufficient or improper scoring. Ensure that your scoring cuts are deep enough to allow for proper expansion of the dough during baking. Experiment with different scoring techniques and angles to find what works best for your bread.

Creative Flavor and Ingredient Additions:

Shaping bread not only allows for artistic expression but also provides an opportunity to incorporate additional flavors and ingredients into your creations. Here are some ways to enhance the flavor and texture of your shaped bread:

a. Filling and Swirls: Add a layer of flavor by incorporating fillings such as cheese, herbs, pesto, caramelized onions, or chocolate into the shaped dough. Roll the dough around the filling, creating beautiful swirls that burst with flavor.

b. Toppings and Seeds: Experiment with different toppings and seeds to add texture and flavor to your bread. Sprinkle sesame seeds, poppy seeds, sunflower seeds, or flaxseeds on the surface of your shaped dough before baking.

c. Herb and Spice Infusions: Infuse your dough with aromatic herbs and spices to create a fragrant and flavorful bread. Consider incorporating ingredients like rosemary, thyme, garlic, cinnamon, or cardamom during the shaping process.

d. Cheese and Nut Coatings: Roll shaped dough in a mixture of grated cheese, finely chopped nuts, or a combination of both. This adds a crunchy crust and an extra layer of flavor to your bread.

The Role of Resting and Proofing:

Resting and proofing play a vital role in shaping bread. After the initial shaping, the dough needs time to relax and proof before baking. Here's why resting and proofing are important:

a. Relaxation of Gluten: Resting the dough allows the gluten to relax, making it easier to handle during the shaping process. This helps prevent the dough from springing back or resisting shaping.

b. Flavor Development: During the resting and proofing stages, the yeast continues to ferment and produce carbon dioxide, which contributes to flavor development. The additional fermentation time allows for more complex flavors to develop in the bread.

c. Final Rise and Expansion: Proofing provides the necessary time for the dough to undergo its final rise. This allows the dough to expand and develop a light, airy crumb and a beautiful shape.

d. Enhanced Oven Spring: Proper proofing ensures that the dough has enough strength and fermentation activity to achieve optimal oven spring. The oven spring refers to the significant rise in the dough during the initial stages of baking.

Embracing Imperfections and Developing Your Style:

While precise shaping and perfect loaves are admirable goals, it's important to embrace the imperfections that may arise along the way. Every loaf you shape is unique and represents your personal touch as the baker. Embrace the rustic charm of artisanal bread and appreciate the character that each loaf carries.

As you continue to practice kneading and shaping, you will develop your own style and signature techniques. Embrace experimentation, learn from your mistakes, and don't be afraid to think outside the box. The artistry of bread is about exploration, creativity, and the joy of creating something both delicious and visually captivating.

Customizing and Adapting Shaping Techniques:
While there are traditional shaping techniques, don't be afraid to customize and adapt them to suit your preferences and creativity. Here are a few ways to customize your shaping techniques:

a. Size and Weight: Experiment with different sizes and weights of bread. You can shape smaller individual rolls, larger loaves for sharing, or even mini versions of classic shapes. Adjust the dough's weight and shaping technique accordingly.

b. Variations in Scoring: Scoring is not only functional but also adds visual appeal to your bread. Try different scoring patterns, depths, or angles to create unique designs and patterns on the bread's surface.

c. Experimental Shapes: Break free from traditional shapes and experiment with unconventional designs. You can create braided wreaths, knotted rolls, or even free-form shapes that allow for artistic expression.

d. Composite Shapes: Combine different shaping techniques to create composite shapes. For example, you can combine a boule with a batard shape, creating a hybrid loaf that showcases the best of both styles.

Beyond Basic Shaping: Filled and Stuffed Breads

Take your shaping skills to the next level by exploring filled and stuffed breads. These creations involve incorporating delicious fillings into the dough before shaping. Here are a few ideas to inspire you:

a. Cheese-Filled Bread: Roll out the dough into a rectangle, sprinkle your favorite shredded cheese evenly over the surface, and then roll the dough tightly into a log. Cut the log into individual rolls or shape it into a loaf, allowing the cheese to melt and ooze as the bread bakes.

b. Sweet-Filled Bread: Indulge your sweet tooth with sweet filled breads. Spread a layer of butter, cinnamon, and sugar over the dough, then roll it up and shape it into a loaf or individual rolls. As it bakes, the filling will caramelize, creating a delectable sweet swirl.

c. Savory Stuffed Rolls: Divide the dough into smaller portions, flatten each portion, and place a spoonful of your favorite savory filling in the center. Fold the dough over the filling, pinch the edges to seal, and shape it into a roll. Options for fillings include pesto, sun-dried tomatoes, olives, or cooked vegetables.

d. Nutella or Fruit-Filled Braids: Roll the dough into a rectangular shape and spread Nutella or your favorite fruit preserves over the surface. Roll the dough into a log, then slice it lengthwise, creating two halves. Twist the two halves together to form a beautiful braided loaf. As it bakes, the filling will melt and infuse the bread with flavor.

Enhancing Aesthetics with Scoring and Toppings:
Scoring and adding toppings to your shaped bread can enhance its aesthetics and flavor. Here are some tips to consider:

a. Scoring Techniques: Experiment with different scoring techniques to create beautiful patterns on the surface of your bread. You can use a sharp knife, a bread lame, or even a razor blade to make the cuts. Try diagonal slashes, parallel lines, or intricate designs to give your bread a unique look.

b. Flour or Seed Dusting: Before baking, dust the surface of your shaped dough with flour or sprinkle seeds such as sesame, poppy, or flaxseeds. This not only adds visual appeal but also adds texture and flavor to the crust.

c. Egg Wash: Brushing your shaped dough with an egg wash can give it a glossy finish and a beautiful golden color. An egg wash can be made by whisking together an egg with a small amount of water or milk.

d. Glazes and Syrups: Consider applying glazes or syrups to your shaped bread for added shine and flavor. Brushing your bread with honey, maple syrup, or a simple sugar syrup can create a delicious and attractive finish.

Practice, Patience, and Creativity:

Kneading and shaping bread requires practice, patience, and a dash of creativity. Don't be discouraged if your first attempts don't turn out exactly as you envisioned. With time and practice, your skills will improve, and you'll gain confidence in your ability to shape beautiful loaves of bread.

Remember to have fun and let your creativity shine. Each loaf you shape is a unique piece of edible art. Embrace the imperfections and enjoy the process of creating something both visually stunning and delicious.

Utilizing Shaping Tools and Accessories:

To further enhance your bread-shaping skills, consider utilizing specialized tools and accessories. These tools can help you achieve precise shapes, create intricate designs, and make the shaping process more efficient. Here are a few examples:

a. Banneton Proofing Baskets: Banneton baskets, also known as proofing baskets, are made from natural materials like cane or rattan. They provide support to the dough during the final rise and help shape it into a desired form. The banneton's pattern also leaves an imprint on the dough, adding a beautiful touch to the final baked loaf.

b. Bread Lame: A bread lame is a scoring tool with a sharp blade attached to a handle. It is used to create decorative patterns on the surface of the bread before baking. The sharp blade allows for precise scoring, giving your bread an artistic and professional look.

c. Dough Scrapers: Dough scrapers are versatile tools that help with shaping, dividing, and lifting dough. They are especially useful when working with sticky or high-hydration dough. They can be used to gently fold and shape the dough without excessive handling, maintaining its structure and texture.

d. Shaping Molds: Shaping molds come in various shapes and sizes and are designed to help achieve consistent and uniform bread shapes. These molds provide support during the final proofing and baking stages, ensuring your bread retains its desired shape and structure.

Exploring Cultural Shaping Traditions:

Bread-shaping techniques vary across different cultures and regions, each with its own unique traditions and styles. Exploring these cultural shaping techniques can broaden your knowledge and open up new possibilities for creative bread-making. Here are a few examples:

a. Bagels: Bagels, a staple in Jewish cuisine, are shaped by forming a dough rope and then joining the ends to create a ring shape. They are typically boiled before baking, resulting in a chewy texture and a shiny crust.

b. Pretzels: Pretzels have a distinctive knotted shape. They are made by rolling the dough into long ropes, crossing them over each other, and then twisting the ends, creating the iconic pretzel shape. After boiling in a baking soda solution, they are baked to achieve a dark golden crust.

c. Focaccia: Focaccia, an Italian flatbread, is often shaped by pressing the dough into a rectangular or round shape, then using your fingertips to create dimples on the surface. The dimples are typically filled with toppings like olive oil, herbs, olives, or cheese before baking.

d. Chinese Steam Buns: Chinese steam buns, also known as baozi, are shaped by rolling out the dough into small circles, placing a filling in the center, and then folding the dough over to seal the filling. These buns are typically steamed, resulting in a soft and fluffy texture.

Showcasing Your Bread Artistry:

Once you've shaped your bread, it's time to showcase your artistry by baking and presenting your creations. Here are a few tips for displaying and presenting your beautifully shaped bread:

a. Proper Baking: Follow the baking instructions for the specific bread recipe you're working with. Pay attention to temperature, baking time, and any specific techniques or steps needed for optimal results.

b. Cooling and Storing: After baking, allow your bread to cool completely on a wire rack. This helps the crust to crisp up and prevents condensation from forming inside the loaf. Once cooled, store your bread in a breathable bag or wrapped in a clean cloth to maintain its freshness.

c. Photography and Sharing: If you're proud of your shaped bread creations, consider capturing them through photography. Share your photos on social media or with fellow baking enthusiasts to inspire and connect with others who share your passion for bread-making.

d. Sharing the Joy: Bread is meant to be enjoyed and shared. Whether it's a family gathering, a dinner party, or a simple meal with loved ones, sharing your beautifully shaped bread brings joy and satisfaction to those around you. Let others experience the artistry and delicious flavors of your creations.

Advanced Shaping Techniques:

For those looking to push the boundaries of bread-shaping, there are advanced techniques that allow for even more intricate and complex designs. These techniques require skill and practice but can result in truly breathtaking bread creations. Here are a few examples:

a. Swirls and Spirals: Create beautiful swirls and spirals by rolling out the dough into a thin rectangle, spreading a filling of your choice (such as cinnamon sugar, pesto, or cheese), and then tightly rolling the dough into a log. Slice the log and arrange the pieces in a spiral pattern before proofing and baking.

b. Basketweave Pattern: This technique involves weaving strips of dough over and under each other to create a basket-like pattern. It requires precision and careful manipulation of the dough strands, resulting in an impressive and visually stunning loaf.

c. Artistic Sculptures: Challenge your creativity by sculpting bread dough into intricate shapes and designs. From braided animals to sculpted flowers, the possibilities are endless. These sculptural breads not only taste delicious but also serve as stunning centerpieces for special occasions.

d. Filled and Shaped Rolls: Take your dinner rolls to the next level by incorporating fillings and shaping them into unique designs. From pinwheels to stuffed knots, these filled and shaped rolls add an element of surprise and excitement to your bread basket.

Exploring Regional and Cultural Variations:

Bread-shaping techniques vary widely across different regions and cultures, each with its own unique traditions and styles. Exploring these variations allows you to expand your repertoire of shaping techniques and discover new flavors and textures. Here are a few examples:

a. Scandinavian Braids: Scandinavian countries are known for their intricate braided breads. From Swedish cinnamon buns to Finnish pulla, these braided loaves showcase the artistry of bread-shaping. Experiment with different braid styles, such as four-strand or six-strand braids, to create stunning Scandinavian-inspired breads.

b. Middle Eastern Flatbreads: Middle Eastern cuisine offers a rich variety of flatbreads, each with its own distinct shaping techniques. From the round pita breads to the elongated lavash, these flatbreads are shaped and baked in unique ways, resulting in breads that are perfect for dipping, wrapping, or stuffing.

c. Mexican Tortillas: Tortillas are a staple in Mexican cuisine and are traditionally shaped by pressing or rolling the dough into thin, round discs. Explore the art of tortilla making and experiment with different grains, such as corn or wheat, to create authentic and flavorful tortillas.

d. Asian Steamed Buns: Asian cuisine is renowned for its steamed buns, such as Chinese baozi and Japanese nikuman. These buns are shaped by rolling the dough into small rounds, filling them with savory or sweet fillings, and then sealing them into beautifully shaped buns. The steaming process results in soft, fluffy, and mouthwatering buns.

Presenting Your Shaped Bread Creations:

Once you have shaped and baked your bread, it's time to present your creations in an appealing and inviting way. Here are some tips for showcasing your shaped bread:

a. Serving Platters: Choose a beautiful serving platter or cutting board to display your bread. This provides a stylish backdrop for your creations and adds a touch of elegance to the presentation.

b. Garnishes and Accompaniments: Enhance the visual appeal of your shaped bread by adding garnishes and accompaniments. Fresh herbs, edible flowers, or a drizzle of olive oil can add a pop of color and make your bread even more enticing.

c. Bread Baskets: If you are serving a variety of breads, consider using a bread basket to hold and display them. This allows guests to easily select their preferred shapes and flavors.

d. Photography: Capture the beauty of your shaped bread creations through photography. Natural lighting, clean backgrounds, and close-up shots can showcase the intricate details and textures of your bread.

Conclusion:

Chapter 7 has explored the artistry of kneading and shaping bread, covering advanced techniques, regional variations, and presenting your shaped bread creations. By mastering these techniques and exploring the diverse world of bread shaping, you can create breads that not only taste delicious but also look stunning.

Remember that shaping bread is a form of creative expression. Embrace the artistry, experiment with different techniques, and let your imagination guide you. The possibilities for shaping bread are limitless, and each creation is an opportunity to showcase your skills and passion for baking.

Chapter 8

The Perfect Crust: Achieving Texture and Color

The crust of a loaf of bread is its crowning glory, providing a delightful texture, flavor, and visual appeal. In Chapter 8, we will delve into the secrets of achieving the perfect crust. We will explore the factors that contribute to crust formation, different crust textures and colors, and techniques to achieve the desired results. Get ready to unlock the secrets to achieving a crust that will make your bread truly remarkable.

The Role of Heat in Crust Formation:

Heat plays a crucial role in the formation of the crust. As the bread bakes, the heat interacts with the dough, resulting in a transformation that creates the characteristic crust we love. Understanding the science behind heat and crust formation will help you achieve the perfect result. Here's how heat affects the crust:

a. Maillard Reaction: The Maillard reaction is a complex chemical reaction that occurs between amino acids and reducing sugars in the dough. It is responsible for the browning and development of flavors in the crust. As the bread bakes, the Maillard reaction intensifies, creating a rich golden-brown crust with a depth of flavor.

b. Caramelization: Caramelization is another important process that takes place during baking. It occurs when sugars in the dough are heated, breaking down and forming new compounds that contribute to the crust's color and flavor. Caramelization adds sweetness and complexity to the crust, enhancing its overall appeal.

c. Evaporation: Heat causes moisture in the dough to evaporate during baking. This moisture loss leads to the development of a crisp and crunchy crust. The evaporation process is essential for achieving the desired texture in the crust.

Understanding Crust Textures:

The texture of the crust can vary significantly depending on factors such as ingredients, baking technique, and desired outcome. Let's explore some common crust textures:

a. Soft Crust: A soft crust is typically achieved by brushing the surface of the dough with a fat, such as butter or oil, before baking. This creates a protective barrier that prevents excessive moisture loss, resulting in a softer and more tender crust.

b. Crispy Crust: A crispy crust is the result of achieving the right balance of moisture loss and browning. It has a thin and crackly exterior that shatters when bitten into. Achieving a crispy crust requires proper baking techniques and understanding the impact of temperature and humidity.

c. Chewy Crust: A chewy crust has a more substantial texture with a bit of resistance when bitten into. It requires a longer baking time and higher oven temperatures to achieve the desired chewiness. Steam during the initial stages of baking can also contribute to a chewy crust by keeping the surface of the dough moist.

d. Crusty Crust: A crusty crust is characterized by its thick, hard exterior that provides a satisfying crunch. It is often achieved by baking at high temperatures, creating a deeply browned and well-developed crust. A combination of steam and prolonged baking helps achieve the desired crusty texture.

Techniques for Achieving the Desired Crust:

a. Steam: Steam is a crucial element in achieving a beautiful crust. It helps create a moist environment during the initial stages of baking, allowing the dough to expand before the crust sets. The steam also delays the formation of a dry skin on the dough's surface, enabling the crust to develop more fully.

Steam Injection Ovens: Professional bakeries often use steam injection ovens, where steam is released at specific intervals during the baking process. This ensures consistent and controlled steam levels, resulting in excellent crust development.

Home Baking Techniques: For home bakers, there are several ways to create steam in a regular home oven. One method is to place a pan of hot water on the bottom rack while preheating the oven. Another method involves spritzing water onto the sides of the oven or onto the dough itself using a spray bottle.

b. Baking Stone or Steel: Using a baking stone or steel in the oven helps to create a more even and intense heat transfer, resulting in a well-developed crust. Preheating the stone or steel before placing the dough on it helps to provide a burst of heat to the dough's bottom, contributing to crust formation.

c. Steam Dome Technique: The steam dome technique involves baking the dough covered with a domed lid or inverted heat-resistant bowl for the first portion of the baking time. This creates a microclimate of steam around the dough, promoting crust development.

d. Overnight Refrigeration: Cold fermentation or overnight refrigeration of the shaped dough allows for a slow and controlled rise. This extended fermentation time enhances flavor development and promotes crust formation during baking.

Controlling Crust Color:

Achieving the desired crust color requires careful control of factors such as oven temperature, baking time, and ingredients. Here are some techniques to consider:

a. Oven Temperature: The temperature at which you bake your bread has a direct impact on its crust color. Higher temperatures, such as 425°F (220°C) or even hotter for artisanal-style bread, result in a darker and more caramelized crust. Lower temperatures, around 375°F (190°C), produce a lighter and softer crust.

b. Baking Time: The duration of baking also affects crust color. A longer baking time allows for more browning and caramelization, resulting in a deeper crust color. Keep an eye on your bread while it bakes and adjust the baking time as needed to achieve the desired color.

c. Sugar Wash: Applying a sugar wash to the surface of the dough before baking can contribute to a darker and glossier crust. Simply brush a mixture of water and sugar onto the dough just before it goes into the oven.

d. Milk or Egg Wash: Brushing the dough with milk or beaten egg creates a glossy and golden-brown crust. The proteins in the milk or egg contribute to browning during baking, resulting in an attractive crust color.

Troubleshooting Common Crust Issues:

Sometimes, despite our best efforts, crust issues may arise. Understanding the potential problems and their solutions will help you troubleshoot and improve your crust results. Here are some common crust-related issues and their possible solutions:

a. Pale Crust: If your crust appears pale and lacks color, it may indicate insufficient oven temperature or baking time. Ensure that your oven is properly preheated to the recommended temperature, and consider extending the baking time to allow for more browning.

b. Thick and Tough Crust: A thick and tough crust may result from excessive baking time or high oven temperatures. To achieve a thinner and more tender crust, reduce the baking time and lower the oven temperature slightly.

c. Soggy Crust: A soggy crust can be the result of excess moisture in the oven or insufficient moisture loss during baking. Ensure that your dough is properly proofed and that the oven is adequately preheated. Additionally, be mindful of using too much steam during the baking process, as excessive moisture can lead to a soggy crust.

d. Uneven Crust Color: Uneven crust color can be caused by uneven heat distribution in the oven. To combat this issue, consider rotating the bread halfway through the baking time or using a baking stone or steel to promote even heat transfer.

Enhancing Flavor and Texture through Toppings:

Toppings can add a delightful flavor and visual appeal to your crust. Here are some popular topping options to try:

a. Seeds: Sprinkling seeds, such as sesame, poppy, or sunflower seeds, onto the dough before baking adds texture and flavor to the crust. These seeds can be used individually or in combination to create your desired topping.

b. Herbs and Spices: Fresh or dried herbs, such as rosemary, thyme, or oregano, can be chopped finely and pressed onto the dough's surface. Spices like garlic powder, onion powder, or paprika can also be used to add a kick of flavor.

c. Sea Salt: Sprinkling a pinch of coarse sea salt onto the dough before baking not only enhances the flavor but also adds a pleasing salty crunch to the crust.

d. Cheese: Grated or crumbled cheese can be sprinkled over the dough to create a flavorful and cheesy crust. Options like Parmesan, cheddar, or feta work well, depending on your bread's flavor profile.

Storing Bread for Optimal Crust:

To maintain the quality of your bread's crust, proper storage is essential. Here are some tips for storing bread to preserve its texture and crust:

a. Cool Completely: Allow your bread time to cool completely on a wire rack before storing. This prevents condensation from forming inside the bag or container, which can lead to a soggy crust.

b. Paper or Bread Bag: Store your bread in a paper bag or a bread-specific storage bag that allows airflow. This helps maintain the crust's crispness and prevents the bread from becoming overly moist.

c. Avoid Plastic Bags: While plastic bags may help retain moisture, they can also make the crust soft and less desirable. If you prefer a softer crust, you can store the bread in a plastic bag but ensure it has cooled completely.

d. Freeze for Long-Term Storage: If you need to store bread for an extended period, consider freezing it. Slice the bread before freezing, allowing you to defrost only the slices you need while keeping the rest frozen. This preserves the crust's texture and flavor.

Enhancing Crust Flavor with Pre-Ferments:

Pre-ferments, such as sourdough starter or poolish, can contribute to the development of a rich and flavorful crust. These pre-ferments not only add complexity to the overall flavor of the bread but also enhance the crust's taste. The longer fermentation process allows for the formation of more aromatic compounds, resulting in a more pronounced and delicious crust.

Using Steam in Home Baking:
While steam injection ovens are commonly used in professional baking, there are ways to generate steam in a regular home oven. Here are some techniques for utilizing steam in home baking:

a. Water Pan: Place a pan filled with hot water on the bottom rack of the oven during preheating. The water will evaporate, creating a steamy environment that promotes crust development. Be cautious when adding water to a hot oven to avoid potential steam burns.

b. Spritzing Method: Use a spray bottle filled with water to spritz the sides of the oven or directly onto the dough before placing it in the oven. The moisture from the spritzing will create steam, contributing to a well-developed crust.

c. Ice Cubes: Another method is to place a tray of ice cubes on the bottom rack of the oven during preheating. The ice cubes will melt, releasing steam and creating a humid environment.

The Impact of Oven Temperature and Baking Time:

The oven temperature and baking time significantly influence crust development. Here are some considerations:

a. Higher Temperature: Baking bread at a higher temperature, typically between 425°F (220°C) to 475°F (245°C), promotes a more pronounced crust color and crisp texture. The intense heat helps to caramelize the sugars on the surface, creating a beautiful golden-brown crust.

b. Lower Temperature: Baking at a lower temperature, around 375°F (190°C) to 400°F (200°C), results in a lighter-colored crust with a softer texture. This is ideal for bread that requires a tender crust, such as sandwich loaves or enriched doughs.

c. Baking Time: The baking time is crucial in achieving the desired crust texture and color. Longer baking times allow for more moisture evaporation and caramelization, resulting in a thicker and crunchier crust. Monitor the bread closely during baking to prevent over-browning or burning.

Creating a Shiny Crust with Washes:

Applying a wash to the surface of the dough before baking can create a shiny and attractive crust. Here are some common washes used in bread baking:

a. Egg Wash: Whisk an egg with a small amount of water or milk and brush it onto the surface of the dough. This creates a glossy and golden-brown crust. You can also use just the egg yolk for a richer color or the egg white for a lighter shine.

b. Milk Wash: Brushing milk onto the dough can result in a softer and less shiny crust compared to an egg wash. It adds a subtle richness and enhances the browning process.

c. Water Wash: Brushing plain water onto the dough before baking can create a crisp and slightly shiny crust. It is a simple and effective option if you prefer a more straightforward approach.

Troubleshooting Common Crust Issues:

While striving for that perfect crust, it's essential to troubleshoot and address any potential issues that may arise. Here are some common crust-related problems and their solutions:

a. Pale Crust: If your crust is pale and lacks color, it may indicate insufficient oven temperature or baking time. Ensure that your oven is properly preheated and consider extending the baking time to allow for more browning.

b. Thick and Tough Crust: A thick and tough crust may result from excessive baking time or high oven temperatures. To achieve a thinner and more tender crust, reduce the baking time and lower the oven temperature slightly.

c. Soggy Crust: A soggy crust can be caused by excess moisture during baking or improper cooling and storage. Ensure that your bread is baked until fully cooked and allow it to cool completely on a wire rack before storing.

d. Uneven Crust Color: Uneven crust color can occur due to uneven heat distribution in the oven. To address this issue, rotate the bread halfway through baking or consider using a baking stone or steel for more even heat transfer.

Exploring Different Types of Bread Crusts:

Not all bread crusts are created equal. Different types of breads and baking techniques can result in unique crust characteristics. Let's explore some popular bread crust types:

a. Baguette Crust: Baguettes are known for their crisp and crackly crust. Achieving this type of crust requires a high-temperature bake with steam, along with proper shaping and scoring techniques.

b. Artisanal-Style Crust: Artisanal-style bread often boasts a thick and crusty exterior with a deep golden-brown color. The use of pre-ferments, longer fermentation times, and high-temperature baking contribute to this crust's development.

c. Sandwich Loaf Crust: Sandwich loaves typically have a softer and thinner crust compared to rustic breads. They are often baked at a lower temperature for a shorter time to maintain a softer texture.

d. Sourdough Crust: Sourdough breads feature a tangy and flavorful crust. The use of a sourdough starter and extended fermentation allows for the development of a unique crust that adds depth to the overall flavor profile.

Enhancing Crust Flavor with Toppings:

Adding toppings to the crust can elevate the flavor and appearance of your bread. Here are some popular options to consider:

a. Seeds: Sprinkling sesame seeds, poppy seeds, or sunflower seeds onto the dough before baking can add texture and nuttiness to the crust.

b. Herbs and Spices: Finely chopped fresh or dried herbs like rosemary, thyme, or oregano can infuse the crust with aromatic flavors. Spices such as garlic powder, onion powder, or paprika can also add a punch of taste.

c. Salt Flakes: Sprinkling flaky sea salt on the surface of the dough before baking can create bursts of salty goodness and enhance the overall flavor of the crust.

d. Cheese: Grated or crumbled cheese can be sprinkled over the dough to create a cheesy and flavorful crust. Options like Parmesan, cheddar, or Gruyère work well, depending on the bread's flavor profile.

Proper Storage for Preserving Crust Quality:

To maintain the quality of your bread's crust, proper storage is essential. Follow these tips for preserving crust texture and flavor:

a. Cool Completely: Allow your bread to cool completely on a wire rack before storing. This prevents condensation from forming inside the bag or container, which can lead to a soggy crust.

b. Paper or Bread Bag: Store your bread in a paper bag or a bread-specific storage bag that allows airflow. This helps maintain the crust's crispness and prevents the bread from becoming overly moist.

c. Avoid Plastic Bags: While plastic bags may help retain moisture, they can also make the crust soft and less desirable. If you prefer a softer crust, you can store the bread in a plastic bag but ensure it has cooled completely.

d. Freeze for Long-Term Storage: If you need to store bread for an extended period, consider freezing it. Slice the bread before freezing, allowing you to defrost only the slices you need while keeping the rest frozen. This preserves the crust's texture and flavor.

Innovating with Crust Variations:
Once you have mastered the fundamentals of crust formation, feel free to innovate and experiment with unique crust variations. Here are some ideas to spark your creativity:
a. Flavored Oils: Infuse oils with herbs, spices, or garlic and brush them onto the dough before baking. This imparts additional flavors and adds an extra dimension to the crust.

b. Sourdough Blistered Crust: To achieve a blistered crust, increase the oven temperature during the initial stage of baking and create steam. This technique encourages the formation of distinctive bubbles on the crust surface.

c. Laminated Doughs: Laminated doughs, such as croissants or puff pastry, feature distinct flaky and crispy crust layers. Mastering the technique of layering butter within the dough can result in a show-stopping crust.

d. Decorative Scoring: Experiment with different scoring patterns to create visually appealing crust designs. Play with simple lines, intricate patterns, or even shapes to add an artistic touch to your bread.

We have explored the art and science of achieving the perfect crust. From understanding the role of heat and mastering different crust textures and colors to employing techniques and troubleshooting common issues, you now have the knowledge to create bread with a crust that is both visually appealing and full of flavor.

Remember to experiment, practice, and observe the effects of different variables on crust formation. Each loaf you bake presents an opportunity to refine your crust-making skills and take your bread to new heights.

Chapter 9

Diversifying Your Breads: Exploring Flavors and Ingredients

Here in Chapter 9, we will embark on further culinary adventures as we explore the world of diverse bread flavors and ingredients. Bread is a versatile canvas that can be infused with an array of flavors and textures to suit your taste preferences and culinary creativity. From incorporating herbs and spices to experimenting with different grains and fillings, here we will dive into the art of diversifying your breads. Get ready to expand your baking repertoire and tantalize your tastebuds with exciting new flavors and ingredients!

Harnessing the Power of Herbs and Spices:

Herbs and spices have the ability to elevate the flavor profile of your bread, adding depth and complexity. Here are some popular herbs and spices to consider:

a. Rosemary: Known for its aromatic and piney flavor, rosemary pairs well with savory breads, such as focaccia or rustic loaves.

b. Cinnamon: The warm and comforting notes of cinnamon can enhance sweet breads, like cinnamon rolls or raisin bread.

c. Basil: With its fresh and slightly peppery taste, basil can add a delightful twist to herb-infused breads or tomato-based loaves.

d. Nutmeg: The warm and earthy flavor of nutmeg is a fantastic addition to spiced breads, such as pumpkin or banana bread.

e. Turmeric: This vibrant spice adds a golden hue and subtle earthy notes to breads. It pairs well with flavors like ginger, cardamom, and coconut.

Exploring Specialty Grains and Flours:

Diversify your bread repertoire by incorporating specialty grains and flours. These unique ingredients bring distinct flavors and textures to your baked goods. Here are a few to consider:

a. Whole Wheat Flour: Swap out a portion of all-purpose flour with whole wheat flour to add a nutty flavor and a hearty texture to your bread. It also boosts the nutritional value.

b. Rye Flour: Rye flour imparts a distinct flavor to bread, ranging from mild and earthy to robust and tangy. It is commonly used in traditional rye breads, pumpernickel, and sourdough loaves.

c. Spelt Flour: Spelt flour is an ancient grain that lends a slightly sweet and nutty flavor to bread. It has a lower gluten content compared to wheat flour, resulting in a denser texture.

d. Quinoa Flour: Quinoa flour adds a protein-rich element to bread and contributes a slightly earthy and nutty flavor. It pairs well with other gluten-free flours for baking delicious gluten-free bread.

e. Buckwheat Flour: Despite its name, buckwheat is not related to wheat and is naturally gluten-free. It offers a unique earthy and nutty taste, perfect for hearty breads and pancakes.

Infusing Bread with Fruits and Vegetables:

Fruits and vegetables can impart moisture, natural sweetness, and delightful flavors to your bread. Consider these options:

a. Banana: Mashed ripe bananas are a popular addition to bread, adding natural sweetness and moisture. Banana bread is a classic example of how this fruit can transform a simple loaf into a delicious treat.

b. Zucchini: Grated zucchini adds moisture and a subtle flavor to bread. It works particularly well in quick breads and can be combined with other ingredients like chocolate or nuts.

c. Carrots: Finely grated carrots bring natural sweetness and a vibrant color to bread. Carrot bread, spiced with cinnamon and nutmeg, is a delightful variation.

d. Apples: Chopped or grated apples can lend moisture and a touch of sweetness to bread. Pair them with warm spices like cinnamon or nutmeg for an autumn-inspired treat.

e. Citrus Zest: The zest of citrus fruits, such as lemon, orange, or lime, adds bright and refreshing flavors to bread. It provides a zingy contrast to rich or sweet breads.

Incorporating Cheese, Nuts, and Seeds:

Cheese, nuts, and seeds can transform your bread, adding texture, flavor, and visual appeal. Experiment with the following:

a. Cheese: Grated or cubed cheese can be incorporated into bread dough, creating pockets of melted goodness. Cheddar, Parmesan, or Gruyère are popular choices.

b. Nuts: Toasted and chopped nuts, such as walnuts, almonds, or pecans, can add crunch and a rich, nutty flavor to bread. They work well in both sweet and savory breads.

c. Seeds: Seeds like sesame, poppy, flax, or sunflower seeds can be sprinkled on top of bread or incorporated into the dough. They add texture and a delightful nutty flavor.

Sweet and Savory Fillings:

Inject excitement into your breads by experimenting with sweet and savory fillings. Consider these options:

a. Sweet Fillings: Spread Nutella, cinnamon sugar, or fruit preserves onto the dough before rolling it up to create sweet swirls in bread. You can also add dried fruits, chocolate chips, or caramelized nuts.

b. Savory Fillings: For savory breads, incorporate ingredients like caramelized onions, roasted garlic, sun-dried tomatoes, or olives. Cheese, herbs, and cooked bacon can also add layers of flavor.

Exploring Ethnic Flavors:

Embrace the rich culinary heritage of different cultures by infusing your bread with ethnic flavors. Here are some ideas to inspire you:

a. Indian Spices: Incorporate spices like cumin, coriander, turmeric, or garam masala into your dough for an Indian-inspired bread. It pairs well with lentils, chickpeas, or paneer fillings.

b. Mediterranean Flavors: Use ingredients like olives, feta cheese, sun-dried tomatoes, and oregano to create a Mediterranean-inspired bread bursting with robust flavors.

c. Asian Influences: Infuse your bread with Asian flavors by adding ingredients such as sesame oil, soy sauce, ginger, or lemongrass. Fillings like teriyaki chicken or stir-fried vegetables can create a delightful fusion bread.

d. Middle Eastern Delights: Incorporate spices like za'atar, sumac, or cardamom into your bread for a Middle Eastern twist. Fillings such as spiced ground lamb, feta cheese, or roasted eggplant can add depth of flavor.

Gluten-Free and Alternative Bread Options:

For those following a gluten-free diet or seeking alternative options, there are numerous possibilities for creating delicious bread. Consider these alternatives:

a. Gluten-Free Flours: Explore gluten-free flours like almond flour, coconut flour, rice flour, or a gluten-free flour blend to create bread with unique flavors and textures.

b. Psyllium Husk: Adding psyllium husk to gluten-free bread dough can improve its texture and structure. It acts as a binder and helps retain moisture.

c. Legume Flours: Flours made from legumes like chickpeas or lentils offer a protein-rich alternative for gluten-free bread. They can be used alone or in combination with other gluten-free flours.

d. Sourdough Starter: Gluten-free sourdough bread made with a gluten-free starter offers a tangy flavor and improved texture compared to traditional gluten-free bread.

Incorporating Exotic Flavors:

Expand your flavor horizons by incorporating exotic ingredients into your bread. Here are some examples:

a. Matcha: The vibrant and earthy flavor of matcha green tea powder can add a unique twist to your bread. Use it sparingly to create a subtly infused bread with a beautiful green hue.

b. Lavender: Dried lavender flowers can infuse your bread with a delicate floral aroma and flavor. Pair it with lemon zest for a delightful combination.

c. Saffron: Known for its rich and luxurious flavor, saffron can impart a golden color and a subtle floral taste to your bread. It works particularly well in sweet breads like brioche.

d. Cardamom: This aromatic spice adds a warm and slightly citrusy flavor to bread. It is a staple in Scandinavian baking and pairs well with flavors like cinnamon and orange.

Gluten-Free and Alternative Bread Options:

For those with dietary restrictions or preferences, there are various gluten-free and alternative bread options available. Explore the following:

a. Nut-Based Breads: Utilize ground almonds, cashews, or hazelnuts as the base for your bread dough. These nut flours provide a unique flavor and a moist texture to your gluten-free bread.

b. Seed-Based Breads: Experiment with breads made from seeds like flaxseeds, chia seeds, or sunflower seeds. These seeds are rich in fiber and healthy fats, creating bread with a satisfying crunch.

c. Vegetable-Based Breads: Incorporate vegetables like cauliflower, zucchini, or sweet potato into your bread dough. These vegetables not only add moisture but also contribute to the overall flavor and nutritional value.

d. Legume-Based Breads: Explore breads made from legumes such as chickpeas, lentils, or black beans. These legume flours are high in protein and fiber, making them an excellent alternative to traditional wheat bread.

Exploring Bread Cultures:

Bread is a staple in many cultures around the world, each with its own unique flavors and techniques. Embrace the diversity of bread cultures by trying out different recipes and traditions:

a. French Bread: Delve into the world of French bread with classics like baguettes, pain de mie, or brioche. Experiment with shaping techniques, crust variations, and regional specialties.

b. Italian Bread: Explore the rich traditions of Italian bread, including ciabatta, focaccia, and panettone. Learn about the importance of olive oil, herbs, and regional specialties like Tuscan bread or Sicilian pizza dough.

c. Indian Bread: Discover the variety of Indian breads, such as naan, paratha, or dosa. Experiment with Indian spices, fillings, and accompaniments to create a fusion of flavors in your bread.

d. Scandinavian Bread: Experience the simplicity and wholesome nature of Scandinavian bread, including rye bread, knäckebröd, or cardamom-infused loaves. Explore their unique shaping techniques and flavor combinations.

Unconventional Baking Methods:

Expand your baking repertoire by exploring unconventional methods of bread baking. Consider these techniques:

a. Dutch Oven Baking: Baking bread in a preheated Dutch oven creates a steamy environment, resulting in a crusty exterior and a soft, moist crumb. This technique is particularly effective for rustic, artisanal-style breads.

b. Grilling or Barbecuing Bread: Grilling or barbecuing bread gives it a smoky and charred flavor, perfect for summer gatherings or adding a unique twist to your bread.

c. Slow Fermentation: Explore the art of slow fermentation, allowing your dough to rise and develop flavor over an extended period. This method enhances the complexity and depth of your bread's taste.

d. Wood-Fired Oven Baking: If you have access to a wood-fired oven, consider using this traditional method to bake your bread. The intense heat and smoky aroma impart a unique character to your loaves.

Fermentation Techniques:

Fermentation plays a vital role in breadmaking, adding depth of flavor and complexity. Explore different fermentation techniques to enhance the taste of your bread:

a. Sourdough Fermentation: Dive into the world of sourdough bread, where natural wild yeast and lactobacilli cultures create a tangy and distinctive flavor profile. Experiment with different sourdough starters and varying fermentation times for unique results.

b. Poolish or Biga: Poolish and biga are pre-ferments that involve mixing a portion of the flour, water, and yeast to create a bubbly and flavorful base. Incorporating these pre-ferments into your bread dough adds complexity and a slightly tangy taste.

c. Overnight Refrigeration: Allow your bread dough to ferment slowly in the refrigerator overnight. This extended fermentation time enhances the flavor development and results in a richer and more pronounced taste.

d. Autolyse Method: Autolyse is a technique where the flour and water are mixed and left to rest for a period before adding the yeast or sourdough starter. This helps develop gluten and improves the overall flavor of the bread.

Exploring Sweet Breads:

While bread is most often associated with savory flavors, sweet breads offer a delightful alternative. Explore the world of sweet breads with these delectable options:

a. Cinnamon Rolls: Indulge in the warm and comforting flavors of cinnamon rolls. These soft and gooey treats are perfect for breakfast or a special dessert.

b. Babka: Originating from Eastern Europe, babka is a sweet, twisted bread filled with flavors like chocolate, cinnamon, or fruit. Its beautiful swirls and rich taste make it an impressive centerpiece for any occasion.

c. Challah: Dive into the Jewish tradition with challah bread, known for its rich and slightly sweet taste. It's often braided, making it visually stunning and perfect for celebratory occasions.

d. Brioche: Discover the buttery and tender delight of brioche bread. Its high butter and egg content give it a rich flavor and a soft, luxurious texture.

Gluten-Free Breads:

For those with gluten sensitivities or dietary restrictions, gluten-free bread options provide a way to still enjoy delicious homemade bread. Explore gluten-free alternatives with these suggestions:

a. Gluten-Free Flour Blends: Utilize pre-made gluten-free flour blends that combine different gluten-free flours for a well-balanced texture and flavor. Experiment with different blends to find the one that suits your taste.

b. Xanthan Gum or Psyllium Husk: Adding a small amount of xanthan gum or psyllium husk to gluten-free bread dough helps improve its texture, structure, and moisture retention.

c. Nut and Seed Flours: Explore the versatility of nut and seed flours, such as almond flour, coconut flour, or ground flaxseeds. These flours offer a nutrient-rich base for gluten-free bread and add a distinct flavor.

d. Gluten-Free Sourdough: Dive into the world of gluten-free sourdough, using alternative flours like rice flour, buckwheat flour, or sorghum flour. Gluten-free sourdough offers a tangy taste and improved texture in gluten-free bread.

Gluten-Free and Alternative Grains:

For those with gluten sensitivities or dietary preferences, exploring gluten-free and alternative grains opens up a world of possibilities. Consider the following options:

a. Buckwheat: Despite its name, buckwheat is not related to wheat and is naturally gluten-free. It has a unique nutty flavor and can be used in bread recipes, pancakes, or even as a base for gluten-free sourdough.

b. Teff: Teff is a small grain native to Ethiopia and is rich in nutrients. It has a mild, nutty flavor and can be used to make gluten-free breads and flatbreads.

c. Millet: Millet is a versatile grain that can be ground into flour and used in gluten-free baking. It has a slightly sweet and nutty flavor and pairs well with a variety of ingredients.

d. Quinoa: Quinoa is a complete protein grain that can be ground into flour or used as whole grains in bread recipes. It adds a delicate nutty flavor and a pleasant texture to gluten-free bread.

e. Amaranth: Amaranth is a nutritious grain that can be used in gluten-free baking. It has a slightly earthy and nutty flavor, making it a great addition to bread recipes.

Flavorful Bread Enhancements:

Enhancing the flavor of your bread can be done through various additions and enhancements. Consider the following options:

a. Toasted Seeds: Toasted sesame seeds, poppy seeds, or sunflower seeds can be sprinkled on top of your bread to add a delightful crunch and nutty flavor.

b. Dried Fruits: Chopped dried fruits such as raisins, cranberries, or apricots can add bursts of sweetness and texture to your bread. Soak them in warm water or juice before adding them to the dough to prevent them from drying out the bread.

c. Herbs and Spices: Experiment with different herbs and spices to infuse your bread with unique flavors. Rosemary, thyme, oregano, cinnamon, or even chili flakes can add depth and complexity to your bread.

d. Cheese: Incorporating grated or crumbled cheese into your bread dough can result in a savory and indulgent treat. Cheddar, Parmesan, or Gruyère are popular choices that complement a wide range of bread flavors.

e. Sweeteners: Enhance the sweetness of your bread by using natural sweeteners like honey, maple syrup, or molasses. These sweeteners not only add flavor but also contribute to the overall moisture and texture of the bread.

Exploring Regional Bread Specialties:

Bread is deeply rooted in various regional traditions, and exploring regional specialties can offer a glimpse into unique flavor profiles. Consider these regional bread specialties:

a. Bagels: Dive into the world of New York-style bagels or experiment with different variations like Montreal-style bagels. These chewy, dense rings of bread are perfect for toasting and slathering with cream cheese or your favorite toppings.

b. Focaccia: Originating from Italy, focaccia is a flatbread that can be flavored with various toppings such as olives, rosemary, tomatoes, salt or caramelized onions. It has a tender and light texture, making it ideal for sandwiches or as an accompaniment to soups and salads.

c. Pretzels: Explore the traditional German pretzels, with their distinctive knot shape and chewy texture. Whether coated in coarse salt or paired with mustard, pretzels offer a unique flavor and a satisfying snack.

d. Bannock: Dive into indigenous cuisine with bannock, a traditional bread originating from Indigenous cultures. Bannock can be fried, baked, or cooked over an open fire and offers a delicious and versatile bread option.

e. Pita Bread: Transport yourself to the Mediterranean with homemade pita bread. These round, pocketed breads are perfect for filling with falafel, hummus, or your favorite sandwich fillings.

Chapter 10

Bread for Every Meal: Baking for Breakfast, Lunch, Dinner and Dessert

In this chapter, we will explore the versatility of bread as a staple for every meal of the day. From hearty breakfast options to satisfying lunches and delectable dinner accompaniments, bread offers endless possibilities for creating delicious and fulfilling meals. Join us as we dive into the world of baking for breakfast, lunch, and dinner, discovering new recipes and ideas to elevate your culinary creations.

Rise and Shine with Breakfast Breads:

Breakfast is the perfect time to enjoy the comforting aroma and taste of freshly baked bread. Explore these breakfast bread options:

a. Classic Toast: Start your day with a slice of freshly toasted bread. Whether it's a crusty baguette, whole grain loaf, or a slice of homemade brioche, toasted bread provides a simple and satisfying breakfast option.

b. Fluffy Pancakes: Transform your bread dough into fluffy pancakes by adding a touch of sweetness and your favorite mix-ins, such as blueberries, chocolate chips, or bananas. Serve them with a drizzle of maple syrup or a dollop of yogurt for a delightful breakfast treat.

c. Sweet Rolls: Indulge in decadent cinnamon rolls, sticky buns, or fruit-filled sweet rolls. These soft and gooey delights are perfect for a special breakfast occasion or weekend brunch.

d. Savory Breakfast Sandwiches: Use your homemade bread as a base for savory breakfast sandwiches. Layer it with scrambled eggs, crispy bacon, cheese, and your choice of vegetables for a filling and satisfying start to your day.

Wholesome Lunchtime Options:

Bread is a versatile and convenient option for creating wholesome and satisfying lunches. Consider these ideas:

a. Sandwiches and Wraps: Create an array of delicious sandwiches and wraps using your favorite bread. Whether it's a classic club sandwich, a Mediterranean-inspired wrap, or a veggie-packed sub, bread forms the foundation for a satisfying and portable lunch.

b. Savory Tarts and Quiches: Use bread dough as a base for savory tarts and quiches. Fill it with a variety of ingredients like vegetables, cheese, herbs, and proteins for a hearty and flavorful lunchtime meal.

c. Bread Bowls: Hollow out a round loaf of bread to create a bread bowl. Fill it with hearty soups, stews, or chili for a comforting and complete meal.

d. Flatbreads and Pizzas: Get creative with flatbreads and pizzas by using your bread dough as a base. Top it with your favorite ingredients, such as fresh vegetables, meats, and cheeses, to create a customized lunchtime delight.

Bread as a Dinner Accompaniment:

Bread is an essential accompaniment to many dinner dishes, offering a warm and comforting element to the meal. Consider these options:

a. Dinner Rolls: Bake a batch of soft and fluffy dinner rolls to accompany your evening meal. Brush them with melted butter or sprinkle them with herbs for added flavor.

b. Garlic Bread: Transform a loaf of bread into garlic bread by infusing it with garlic, butter, and herbs. This aromatic and flavorful side dish pairs well with pasta dishes, soups, and stews.

c. Flatbread Pizzas: Create personalized flatbread pizzas with your choice of toppings. Whether you prefer a classic Margherita or a loaded meat and veggie combination, flatbread pizzas offer endless possibilities for a delicious dinner option.

d. Bread Stuffing: Use your homemade bread to make a flavorful stuffing for holiday dinners or as a side dish to accompany roasted meats. Combine bread cubes with herbs, vegetables, and spices for a savory and aromatic stuffing.

Sweet Breads for Dessert:

Bread can even be the star of your dessert menu. Explore these sweet bread options:

a. Bread Pudding: Repurpose stale bread into a luscious bread pudding. Soak the bread in a mixture of milk, eggs, sugar, and your favorite flavors like vanilla, cinnamon, or chocolate. Bake it until golden and serve it warm with a drizzle of caramel sauce or a scoop of ice cream.

b. French Toast: Turn your bread slices into a decadent French toast breakfast or dessert. Dip the bread in a mixture of eggs, milk, and vanilla, then cook it on a griddle until golden brown. Serve it with fresh fruits, powdered sugar, and a drizzle of maple syrup.

c. Bread-Based Dessert Soufflés: Transform bread into a delightful dessert soufflé by combining it with eggs, sugar, and your choice of flavorings like chocolate, berries, or citrus. Bake it until puffed and golden for an impressive sweet treat.

d. Bread-Based Cakes and Muffins: Utilize your bread dough to create cakes and muffins with unique flavors and textures. Incorporate fruits, nuts, or spices to add depth and sweetness to your baked goods.

Bread-Based Appetizers:

Bread can also shine as a versatile ingredient in appetizers. Consider these bread-based appetizer ideas:

a. Bruschetta: Toasted slices of bread topped with a flavorful mixture of tomatoes, garlic, basil, and olive oil make for a refreshing and light appetizer.

b. Crostini: Thin slices of toasted bread can be topped with a variety of delicious ingredients, such as creamy cheeses, cured meats, roasted vegetables, or even seafood.

c. Breaded and Fried: Transform bread into crispy and irresistible appetizers by breading and frying. From breaded mozzarella sticks to crispy breaded mushrooms, these finger foods are sure to impress your guests.

d. Mini Sandwiches: Use small rolls or slices of bread to create bite-sized sandwiches filled with an assortment of ingredients like cured meats, cheeses, spreads, and vegetables. Perfect for serving as finger food at cocktail parties or social gatherings.

Bread-Based Side Dishes:

Bread can play a supporting role as a delightful side dish. Consider these options:

a. Breadsticks: Bake your homemade breadsticks and serve them alongside pasta dishes or soups. These crisp and flavorful sticks are perfect for dipping and adding a touch of elegance to your meal.

b. Focaccia Bread: Enjoy a slice of herb-infused focaccia bread as a side to accompany main courses or as a delicious appetizer. Focaccia can be topped with various ingredients like olives, cherry tomatoes, herbs, or even caramelized onions.

c. Stuffings and Dressings: Utilize bread to create savory stuffings or dressings for holiday meals or special occasions. Combine bread cubes with herbs, vegetables, and broth for a flavorful side dish that complements roasted meats.

d. Bread-Based Salads: Add crunch and texture to your salads by incorporating croutons or toasted bread cubes. Whether it's a panzanella salad with tomatoes and cucumbers or a Caesar salad with homemade garlic croutons, bread adds an extra layer of satisfaction to your greens.

Bread and Sourdough Mastery

Bread as a Base for Tartines and Open-Faced Sandwiches:

Create beautiful and flavorful tartines and open-faced sandwiches using bread as a canvas. Explore these ideas:

a. Avocado Toast: Top toasted bread with creamy mashed avocado, a sprinkle of salt and pepper, and additional toppings like sliced tomatoes, poached eggs, or microgreens for a healthy (and trendy) breakfast or brunch option.

b. Smørrebrød: Embrace the Danish tradition of smørrebrød by layering slices of bread with various spreads, pickled vegetables, cured meats, or seafood. These open-faced sandwiches are as visually appealing as they are delicious.

c. Mediterranean Tartines: Spread hummus, tzatziki, or pesto on bread and layer it with ingredients like grilled vegetables, feta cheese, olives, or roasted red peppers for a Mediterranean-inspired tartine bursting with flavors.

d. Bruschetta-Style Tartines: Combine the classic bruschetta flavors with a tartine twist. Top bread with fresh tomato salsa, mozzarella cheese, basil leaves, and a drizzle of balsamic glaze for a delightful appetizer or light lunch option.

Bread-Based Dessert Variations:

In addition to sweet breads mentioned earlier, here are further dessert variations to explore:

a. Bread Pudding Variations: Experiment with different flavors and ingredients in your bread pudding, such as adding chocolate chips, dried fruits, nuts, or a splash of your favorite liqueur for a decadent twist.

b. Bread-Based Ice Cream Sandwiches: Sandwich a scoop of your favorite ice cream between two slices of bread or use sweet buns for a fun and nostalgic treat. Roll the edges in sprinkles, crushed nuts, or chocolate chips for an extra touch of indulgence.

c. Bread-Based Trifles: Layer torn pieces of bread with fruit compotes, custard, whipped cream, and other delectable fillings to create beautiful and satisfying trifles.

d. Bread-Based Puddings: Explore different bread-based pudding recipes, such as rice pudding, bread and butter pudding, or even bread-based chocolate puddings. These comforting desserts are perfect for cozy evenings or special occasions.

Bread-Based Brunch Ideas:

Brunch is a delightful combination of breakfast and lunch, and bread plays a starring role in many brunch dishes. Consider these bread-based brunch ideas:

a. Eggs Benedict: Elevate your brunch game with a classic Eggs Benedict. Toast an English muffin, top it with a poached egg, Canadian bacon or smoked salmon, and Hollandaise sauce for a (decadent!) and satisfying dish.

b. Quiche and Frittatas: Bake a savory quiche or frittata using bread as the crust or as a base for the egg mixture. Add a variety of fillings like cheese, vegetables, and proteins for a delicious and substantial brunch option.

c. French Toast Casserole: Transform slices of bread into a delectable French toast casserole by soaking them in an egg and milk mixture overnight. Bake it the next morning for a sweet and indulgent brunch treat.

d. Monte Cristo Sandwich: Create a savory and satisfying Monte Cristo sandwich by layering slices of bread with ham, turkey, Swiss cheese, and then dipping the assembled sandwich in beaten eggs before grilling or frying it to perfection.

Bread-Based Dips and Spreads:

Bread acts as the perfect vehicle for flavorful dips and spreads. Consider these options:

a. Artichoke and Spinach Dip: Combine cream cheese, artichoke hearts, spinach, and seasonings to create a creamy and flavorful dip. Serve it warm with toasted bread slices or breadsticks for a crowd-pleasing appetizer.

b. Hummus and Baba Ganoush: Whip up a batch of homemade hummus or baba ganoush, both delicious Middle Eastern dips made from chickpeas or roasted eggplant, respectively. Serve them with warm pita bread or slices of crusty bread for a delightful snack or appetizer.

c. Bruschetta Toppings: Create an array of bruschetta toppings using ingredients like fresh tomatoes, basil, mozzarella, roasted red peppers, or a variety of spreads like pesto or tapenade. Serve them on toasted bread slices for a colorful and flavorful appetizer.

d. Cheese Spreads: Mix together your favorite cheeses with herbs, spices, or other flavorings to create delicious spreads. From classic cheddar and garlic spread to creamy brie with cranberry, these spreads pair beautifully with bread or crackers.

Bread-Based Pizzas and Flatbreads:

Bread can be the foundation for homemade pizzas and flatbreads, allowing you to customize your flavors and toppings. Consider these ideas:

a. Margherita Pizza: Top a thin crust or flatbread with fresh tomatoes, mozzarella cheese, basil leaves, and a drizzle of olive oil for a classic Margherita pizza that celebrates simplicity and flavor.

b. Mediterranean Flatbread: Spread hummus or tzatziki on a flatbread and top it with ingredients like grilled chicken, olives, feta cheese, and fresh vegetables for a Mediterranean-inspired delight.

c. Barbecue Chicken Pizza: Brush a pizza crust or flatbread with barbecue sauce and top it with cooked chicken, red onions, and a blend of cheeses for a tangy and savory pizza experience.

d. Veggie Delight: Load your pizza or flatbread with an assortment of fresh vegetables like bell peppers, onions, mushrooms, spinach, and tomatoes for a colorful and nutritious meal option.

Bread-Based Casseroles and Bakes:

Bread can form the base for hearty casseroles and bakes that make for satisfying meals. Consider these options:

a. Bread Pudding Casserole: Transform leftover bread into a savory bread pudding casserole by combining it with ingredients like cheese, vegetables, and cooked meats. Add eggs and milk to create a custard-like mixture, then bake it until golden and set for a comforting and delicious meal.

b. Breakfast Strata: Layer bread, cheese, and various fillings like cooked bacon, sausage, vegetables, or herbs in a baking dish. Pour an egg and milk mixture over the layers and refrigerate it overnight. Bake it the next morning for a flavorful and filling breakfast casserole.

c. Italian Bread Lasagna: Substitute traditional lasagna noodles with slices of bread for a unique twist on this classic Italian dish. Layer bread, meat sauce, cheese, and other fillings, then bake until bubbly and golden for a satisfying dinner option.

d. Bread-Based Mac and Cheese: Combine cooked pasta, cheese sauce, and cubed bread in a baking dish. Top it with more cheese and breadcrumbs, then bake until golden and bubbly for a comforting and indulgent mac and cheese casserole.

Bread-Based Soups and Stews:

Bread can be used as an ingredient or accompaniment to hearty soups and stews. Consider these ideas:

a. Bread Bowls: Hollow out a round loaf of bread and use it as a bowl to serve thick and flavorful soups or stews. The bread absorbs the flavors of the soup, adding an extra layer of deliciousness to each spoonful.

b. Bread Dumplings: Mix bread crumbs, eggs, herbs, and seasonings to form dough. Shape the dough into small dumplings and drop them into simmering soups or stews. The dumplings absorb the flavors of the broth, making delightful and hearty additions to your meal.

c. Croutons: Cut stale bread into cubes, toss them with olive oil, herbs, and seasonings, then bake until golden and crispy. Sprinkle them over your favorite soups or stews for added texture and flavor.

Bread-Based Tacos and Wraps:

Bread can be used as an alternative to tortillas for creating unique and flavorful tacos and wraps. Consider these options:

a. Naan Bread Tacos: Use soft and fluffy naan bread as a base for creating flavorful tacos. Fill them with grilled meats, vegetables, and your choice of toppings like salsa, guacamole, and sour cream.

b. Pita Bread Wraps: Stuff pita bread with a variety of fillings like falafels, grilled chicken, or roasted vegetables. Add a drizzle of tzatziki sauce or your favorite dressing for a satisfying and portable meal.

c. Flatbread Tacos: Use thin flatbread as a shell for creating flavorful and creative tacos. Fill them with seasoned ground meat, crispy vegetables, and your favorite sauces or salsas for a fun and delicious twist on traditional tacos.

Bread-Based Dessert Pizzas:

Who says pizza is only a savory dish? Create dessert pizzas using bread as the base for a sweet and indulgent treat. Consider these ideas:

a. Fruit and Nut Pizza: Spread a sweetened cream cheese or mascarpone mixture on a toasted bread base. Top it with an assortment of fresh fruits like berries, sliced peaches, or kiwi. Sprinkle with chopped nuts and drizzle with honey for a delightful dessert pizza.

b. Chocolate-Hazelnut Pizza: Spread a layer of chocolate-hazelnut spread on a toasted bread base. Top it with sliced bananas, toasted hazelnuts, and a dusting of powdered sugar for a decadent and satisfying dessert option.

c. Cinnamon Sugar Pizza: Sprinkle a mixture of cinnamon and sugar on a toasted bread base. Drizzle it with melted butter and bake until crispy. Serve it with a scoop of vanilla ice cream or a dollop of whipped cream for a delightful cinnamon-sugar dessert pizza.

Whether you're indulging in a slice of toast for breakfast, enjoying a sandwich for lunch, savoring dinner accompaniments like garlic bread, or satisfying your sweet tooth with bread-based desserts, bread will elevate your meals, adding a comforting and delicious element.

With the ideas and recipes provided in this chapter, you now have the blueprint to create memorable and flavorful dishes using bread as the star ingredient. Get creative, experiment with flavors and combinations, and let bread take center stage in your culinary creations.

As we conclude this comprehensive cookbook, we hope it has inspired you to explore the possibilities of baking for breakfast, lunch, and dinner. Embrace the art of bread-making and enjoy the hearty satisfaction of nourishing yourself and your loved ones with homemade bread-based meals.

Happy baking and bon appétit!

Chapter 11

Preserving and Storing: Maximizing the Life of Your Breads

In this chapter, we will delve into the important topic of preserving and storing your bread to maximize its freshness and extend its shelf life. Proper storage techniques are crucial to maintain the quality, texture, and flavor of your homemade bread. Join us as we explore the best practices for preserving and storing bread, ensuring that your delicious baked creations stay fresh and tasty for as long as possible.

Cooling and Resting:

After removing your bread from the oven, it's essential to allow it to cool completely before storing. This cooling process helps the bread set and retain its moisture. Place the bread on a wire rack, allowing air to circulate around it, preventing condensation and ensuring an even cooling process. Avoid cutting into the bread until it has fully cooled, as this can lead to moisture loss.

Wrapping Techniques:

Choosing the right wrapping technique is vital in preserving the freshness and texture of your bread. Consider the following options:

a. Plastic Wrap: Wrap your cooled bread tightly in plastic wrap. Ensure that all exposed surfaces are covered to prevent air from reaching the bread. This method works well for softer bread varieties, like sandwich loaves.

b. Foil: Aluminum foil can be used to wrap your bread, providing a protective barrier against air and moisture. It's especially useful for crusty bread varieties like baguettes or artisanal loaves.

c. Bread Bags: Use specialized bread bags designed to allow excess moisture to escape while protecting the bread from drying out. These bags help maintain the crust's crispness while preventing the bread from becoming stale.

Bread Boxes:

Bread boxes are designed to provide an ideal environment for storing bread. These containers are typically made of wood or metal and feature ventilation holes or slits that allow air circulation while protecting the bread from excessive moisture or dryness. Bread boxes are especially effective in maintaining the crust's crispness and preventing mold growth.

Freezing Bread:

Freezing bread is an excellent option for long-term storage, allowing you to enjoy homemade bread even weeks—or months—later. Follow these steps for successful freezing:

a. Slice or Loaf: Decide whether to freeze your bread in whole loaves or sliced portions, depending on your preference and intended usage. Slicing the bread before freezing allows for easier portioning and thawing.

b. Wrap: Wrap the bread tightly in plastic wrap or aluminum foil to prevent freezer burn and moisture loss. Consider using an additional layer of protection, such as a resealable freezer bag, for extra insulation.

c. Label and Date: Clearly label the wrapped bread with the date of freezing. This information helps you keep track of the bread's freshness and ensures you use the oldest bread first.

d. Freezer Storage: Place the wrapped bread in the freezer, ensuring it's positioned away from any items that could crush or flatten it. It's best to freeze bread in a single layer initially before stacking it to prevent deformation.

e. Thawing: When ready to enjoy your frozen bread, remove the desired portion from the freezer and let it thaw at room temperature. Avoid microwaving the bread for defrosting, as it can lead to uneven thawing and affect the bread's texture.

Reviving Stale Bread:

Sometimes, bread may become stale before you have a chance to consume it. Revive your stale bread with these simple techniques:

a. Oven Refreshing: Preheat your oven to a low temperature, around 300°F (150°C). Sprinkle a little water over the bread's crust to add moisture. Place the bread in the oven for a few minutes until it becomes warm and slightly crisp. This method can help restore some of the bread's freshness.

b. Toasting: Toasting stale bread can help revive its texture and enhance its flavor. Slice the bread and toast it until it becomes golden and crispy. The toasting process removes excess moisture, giving the bread a pleasant crunch.

c. Bread Pudding or Croutons: Transform stale bread into delicious bread pudding or homemade croutons. Soak the bread in a custard mixture for bread pudding or cut it into cubes for croutons. These creations make for tasty alternatives to traditional bread consumption.

Best Practices for Different Bread Types:

Different bread varieties require specific storage techniques to retain their optimal freshness. Consider the following guidelines:

a. Crusty Bread: Crusty bread, like baguettes or artisanal loaves, should be stored at room temperature for up to two days. After that, it's best to wrap it in foil and freeze for longer storage.

b. Soft Sandwich Bread: Soft bread varieties, such as sandwich loaves, can be stored at room temperature for a few days, tightly wrapped in plastic wrap or placed in a bread box. For longer storage, freezing is recommended.

c. Sourdough Bread: Sourdough bread is known for its long shelf life due to its natural acidity. It can be stored at room temperature for up to a week, wrapped in foil or placed in a bread box. Freezing is also an option for longer-term storage.

d. Sweet Breads: Sweet breads, such as banana bread or cinnamon swirl bread, should be stored in airtight containers at room temperature for a few days. They can also be frozen for extended storage.

Monitoring and Discarding:

Regularly monitor your stored bread to ensure it remains fresh and mold-free. Inspect the bread for any signs of mold, excessive dryness, or spoilage. If you notice any issues, promptly discard the affected portion or the entire loaf to prevent contamination and maintain food safety.

Tips for Storing Different Types of Breads:

Different types of bread require specific storage methods to maintain their freshness. Let's explore some tips for storing common bread varieties:

a. Whole Grain Breads: Whole grain breads tend to have a shorter shelf life due to their higher fiber content. To keep them fresh, store them in airtight containers or resealable bags at room temperature for up to three days. For longer storage, consider freezing individual slices or loaves.

b. Rye Breads: Rye breads can become stale quickly, so it's important to store them properly. Wrap rye bread tightly in plastic wrap or aluminum foil and store it in the refrigerator to maintain freshness for up to a week. Alternatively, freeze rye bread for longer storage, ensuring it's well-wrapped to prevent freezer burn.

c. Gluten-Free Breads: Gluten-free breads tend to have a softer texture and can dry out more easily. To preserve their moisture, store them in airtight containers or resealable bags at room temperature for up to five days. If needed, freeze gluten-free bread in individual slices for longer-term storage.

d. Homemade Artisanal Breads: Artisanal breads, with their crusty exterior and chewy interior, require special attention to maintain their quality. After cooling, store them in paper bags or bread boxes at room temperature for up to two days. To extend their shelf life, freeze artisanal breads wrapped in foil or plastic wrap.

Avoiding Moisture Issues:

Moisture can greatly affect the freshness and quality of your bread. Here are some tips to avoid moisture-related problems:

a. Avoid Refrigeration: Refrigerating bread can accelerate moisture loss, leading to a dry and stale texture. It's generally best to store bread at room temperature to maintain its desired freshness and texture.

b. Protect Against Excessive Moisture: While it's essential to avoid dryness, excessive moisture can lead to mold growth. Ensure that your bread is fully cooled before wrapping or storing to prevent condensation. If you live in a humid climate, consider using a bread box with ventilation to balance moisture levels.

c. Freeze in Portions: If you frequently freeze bread, portion it into smaller slices or individual servings before freezing. This way, you can thaw only what you need, reducing the risk of refreezing and potential moisture issues.

d. Avoid Cling Wrap: Cling wrap or plastic wrap can trap moisture, causing the bread's crust to become too soft and undesirable. Choose looser wraps or use wax paper as an alternative.

Reviving Stale Bread:

Despite your best efforts, bread may occasionally become stale. Don't despair—here are some techniques to revive it:

a. Sprinkle with Water: Lightly moisten the crust of the stale bread with water, then place it in a preheated oven at a low temperature (around 300°F or 150°C) for a few minutes. The moisture and gentle heat will help rehydrate the bread and restore some of its freshness.

b. Make Bread Crumbs or Croutons: Stale bread can be transformed into breadcrumbs or croutons. Grind the bread in a food processor to make breadcrumbs or cube it to create homemade croutons. These can be used in various recipes or as toppings for soups and salads.

c. Toast or Grill: Toasting or grilling stale bread can revive its texture and add a delicious crispness. Slice the bread and toast it in a toaster or under the broiler until golden brown. Enjoy it as-is, or use it as a base for sandwiches and bruschetta.

d. Bread Pudding: Stale bread is perfect for making bread pudding. Soak the bread in a mixture of milk, eggs, sugar, and your choice of flavorings. Bake it until it becomes a custard-like dessert. Serve warm with a drizzle of sauce or a dollop of whipped cream.

Bread Boxes:
Bread boxes (or bins) are specialized containers designed to store bread and help extend its shelf life. They typically have ventilation holes or slits that allow air circulation while preventing excessive moisture buildup. Bread boxes are made from materials like wood, ceramic, or metal, providing an optimal environment for storing bread at room temperature. They help maintain the bread's texture, crust, and overall freshness for an extended period.

Avoiding Refrigeration:

Refrigerating bread is not always the best option, as it can accelerate the staling process. Cold temperatures cause the starch molecules in bread to crystallize faster, resulting in a dry and stale texture. However, certain bread types, like those with perishable fillings or delicate ingredients, may require refrigeration to maintain their freshness and prevent spoilage. In such cases, store the bread in airtight containers or resealable bags to minimize exposure to cold air and moisture.

Bread Cloths:

Traditional bread cloths or bread bags made from cotton or linen can be used to store bread. These natural fabrics help absorb excess moisture, preventing the bread from becoming soggy or moldy. Wrap the bread in a clean bread cloth or place it in a breathable bread bag before storing it in a cool, dry place. This method allows the bread to breathe while protecting it from dust and maintaining its freshness.

Bread Slicers:

If you enjoy uniformly sliced bread but find it challenging to achieve consistent thickness, a bread slicer can be a handy tool. Bread slicers come in various designs, from simple guides to adjustable models with multiple slicing options. They help you achieve even slices and prevent squishing or deforming the bread. By using a bread slicer, you can maintain the bread's structure and preserve its texture for a longer period.

Bread Clips and Ties:

Properly sealing bread packaging is essential to prevent air exposure and maintain freshness. Bread clips or ties are convenient tools for securely sealing bread bags. These small plastic or metal clips can be easily attached to the open end of the bag, creating an airtight seal. They are reusable and help prevent moisture loss, keeping the bread soft and fresh for an extended time.

Repurposing Stale Bread, (continued):

Stale bread doesn't have to go to waste. Instead of discarding it, consider repurposing it into delicious culinary creations:

a. Croutons: Cut stale bread into cubes, toss them with olive oil, herbs, and spices, then bake them until golden and crispy. These homemade croutons are perfect for adding a crunchy element to salads or soups.

b. Bread Pudding: Transform stale bread into a delectable bread pudding by soaking it in a custard mixture of eggs, milk, sugar, and your favorite flavors. Bake it until it becomes a moist and comforting dessert. Experiment with different ingredients like chocolate, fruits, or spices to create unique variations.

c. French Toast: Stale bread is ideal for making indulgent French toast. Soak the bread slices in a mixture of beaten eggs, milk, and cinnamon, then fry them until golden brown. Serve with your favorite toppings like maple syrup, fresh fruits, or whipped cream.

d. Bread Crumbs: Grind stale bread in a food processor or use a rolling pin to crush it into fine crumbs. These bread crumbs can be used as a versatile ingredient for breading meats, adding texture to casseroles, or as a topping for baked dishes.

Using Bread Bags:

Bread bags are specially designed for storing bread, helping to maintain its freshness and texture. These bags are typically made of food-grade plastic or fabric with micro-perforations that allow the bread to breathe while protecting it from excess moisture and air exposure. Place your bread in a bread bag and securely seal it to keep it fresh for longer periods.

Proper Storage Temperature:

The storage temperature plays a crucial role in preserving the freshness of your bread. Ideally, store bread at room temperature, which is around 68°F to 72°F (20°C to 22°C). Avoid storing bread in areas prone to temperature fluctuations, such as near windows, stovetops, or heating vents, as these can affect its quality. Maintaining a stable storage temperature helps prevent mold growth and staling.

Bread Storage Containers:

Investing in a dedicated bread storage container can help prolong the shelf life of your bread. These containers are designed to regulate moisture levels and provide a stable environment for storing bread. Look for containers with adjustable air vents or built-in bread boards that absorb excess moisture. These containers can be placed on countertops or in pantries, ensuring your bread stays fresh and protected.

Vacuum Sealing:

Vacuum sealing is an effective method for preserving bread's freshness. This technique removes air from the packaging, reducing exposure to oxygen and slowing down the staling process. Use a vacuum sealer machine or a handheld vacuum sealer to remove air from plastic bags or specially designed vacuum-sealable bread bags. Remember to seal the bags tightly to maintain the vacuum seal.

Monitoring and Discarding:

Regularly check your stored bread to ensure its quality and freshness. Inspect the bread for any signs of mold, unusual odors, or texture changes. If you notice any indications of spoilage, promptly discard the affected portion or the entire loaf to prevent contamination. Proper monitoring helps ensure that you consume bread that is safe and enjoyable.

Bread Storage Dos and Don'ts:

To summarize the best practices for bread storage, here are some essential dos and don'ts:

Dos:

Allow the bread to cool completely before storing.
Wrap the bread tightly to prevent air exposure.
Use airtight containers, bread boxes, or specialized bread bags for storage.
Label and date your stored bread to keep track of freshness.
Experiment with different storage methods to find what works best for your bread type.

Don'ts:

Don't refrigerate bread unless necessary for specific bread types.
Don't store bread near strong-smelling foods, as it can absorb odors.
Avoid exposing bread to direct sunlight or high humidity.
Don't overcrowd your storage container, as it can lead to moisture buildup.

Bread Storage Mistakes to Avoid:

To ensure the maximum freshness and quality of your bread, it's essential to avoid common storage mistakes. Here are some mistakes to steer clear of:

a. Storing Bread in the Fridge: While refrigeration can slow down the growth of mold, it can also accelerate the staling process, resulting in dry and less flavorful bread. Refrigeration is best reserved for specific bread types, like those with perishable fillings or ingredients that require cooler temperatures.

b. Storing Bread in Direct Sunlight: Exposure to direct sunlight can cause bread to become stale and dry more quickly. Store your bread in a cool, shaded area away from direct sunlight to maintain its freshness and texture.

c. Keeping Bread in Plastic Bags: While plastic bags can provide a temporary solution for storing bread, they can trap moisture and contribute to the growth of mold. It's best to use breathable materials like paper bags or specialized bread bags that allow the bread to breathe and prevent excess moisture buildup.

d. Storing Bread Near Odorous Foods: Bread easily absorbs odors from its surroundings. Avoid storing bread near strong-smelling foods like onions, garlic, or strong cheeses, as it can impact the flavor and aroma of the bread.

e. Cutting Bread Before Storage: Slicing bread before storage exposes more surface area to air, leading to faster moisture loss and staling. It's best to keep the bread whole until you're ready to consume it. Slice only what you need and wrap the remaining portion tightly to maintain its freshness.

Extending Shelf Life with Bread Enhancers:

There are several natural ingredients you can incorporate into your bread recipes to help extend the shelf life and freshness of your loaves. Consider the following bread enhancers:

a. Honey: Adding honey to your bread dough can help retain moisture and increase its shelf life. Honey acts as a natural humectant, keeping the bread soft and fresh for longer.

b. Vinegar: A small amount of vinegar in your bread recipe can help inhibit mold growth and extend the bread's life. Apple cider vinegar or white vinegar are common options.

c. Potato Flour: Potato flour or mashed potatoes can contribute to a longer shelf life by retaining moisture in the bread. It helps keep the crumb soft and moist over time.

d. Diastatic Malt Powder: Diastatic malt powder, derived from sprouted barley, contains enzymes that improve the bread's texture and promote a longer shelf life. It can be added to your dough for enhanced freshness.

Donating Excess Bread:

If you find yourself with more bread than you can consume or store, consider donating it to local food banks, shelters, or charitable organizations. Many communities have programs that accept surplus food donations, including bread. By sharing your homemade bread with those in need, you not only reduce food waste but also contribute to the well-being of others.

So, we have explored numerous strategies and techniques to preserve and store your bread effectively, maximizing its life and maintaining its quality. By avoiding common storage mistakes, utilizing appropriate containers and wrapping materials, and incorporating bread enhancers, you can extend the freshness of your homemade bread.

Remember to adapt your storage methods to different bread types, and always prioritize freshness and quality. With these insights and tips, you can enjoy your homemade bread for longer periods, reducing waste and savoring its delightful flavors.

Happy baking and successful bread preservation!

Bread and Sourdough Mastery

In this comprehensive bread and sourdough recipe cookbook, we have charted a journey through the art of bread-making and sourdough crafting. From understanding the basics of bread-making to exploring the chemistry of bread and delving into the world of sourdough starters, this book has provided you with a wealth of knowledge and practical guidance.

Through detailed information, step-by-step instructions, and informative insights, you have unlocked the secrets to delicious baking—and the artistry of making bread and sourdough. You have learned how to create your first artisanal loaf, embrace the wild nature of sourdough, achieve the perfect crust, and explore a diverse range of flavors and ingredients.

From baking for breakfast, brunch, lunch, dinner and dessert and preserving your bread for extended enjoyment, you have become a confident baker with a comprehensive understanding of bread and sourdough.

We hope that this book has ignited and stoked your passion for bread-making, empowered you to experiment with different recipes and techniques, and brought the joy of baking beautiful artisanal bread from scratch into your life.

May your kitchen be filled with the wonderful aromas of freshly baked bread, and may each slice bring you satisfaction and delight. Give us each day our daily bread! Happy baking and may your bread always rise to perfection!